THE
CERTAINTY
OF
SPRING

POEMS BY A GUATEMALAN
IN EXILE

Julia Esquivel

translation by

Anne Woehrle

Illustrations by Rini Templeton.

Cover Design: Melanie Guste, RSCJ, and Angela Marney, both of the Center for Educational Design and Communication

Material originally published in Spanish as *Florecerás Guatemala*
© Julia Esquivel Velásquez, published by *Ediciones* CUPSA, 1989.

© 1993 Ecumenical Program on Central America
        and the Caribbean (EPICA)
        1470 Irving St., N.W., Washington, D.C. 20010.
        (202) 332-0292; (202) 332-1184 (fax).

Manufactured in the United States of America.

Library in Congress Cataloging-in-Publication Data

Esquivel, Julia, 1930-
        [Florecerás, Guatemala. English and Spanish]
        The certainty of spring : poems by a Guatemalan in exile /
    Julia Esquivel ; translation by Anne Woehrle.
            p.   cm.
        ISBN 0-918346-11-8
        I. Woehrle, Anne.   II. Title.
        PQ7499.2.R68F4913   1993
        861--dc20   92-35394
                                                            CIP

ISBN 0-918346-11-8

ACKNOWLEDGMENTS FOR THE ENGLISH EDITION

We wish to gratefully acknowledge Sally Hanlon, Alicia Partnoy, Kit Collins and Sara Fahy for their contributions to making the English –language edition of this book possible. Special thanks are due to Anne Woehrle for countless hours of careful translating and to Joyce Hollyday for her encouragement and foreword. We are especially thankful to the Religious of the Sacred Heart and to the Chesapeake Province of the School Sisters of Notre Dame for their generous contributions to this effort and to the Center for Educational Design and Communication for their creative design and consulting.

Minor Sinclair, Margaret Low and Scott Wright
EPICA editors

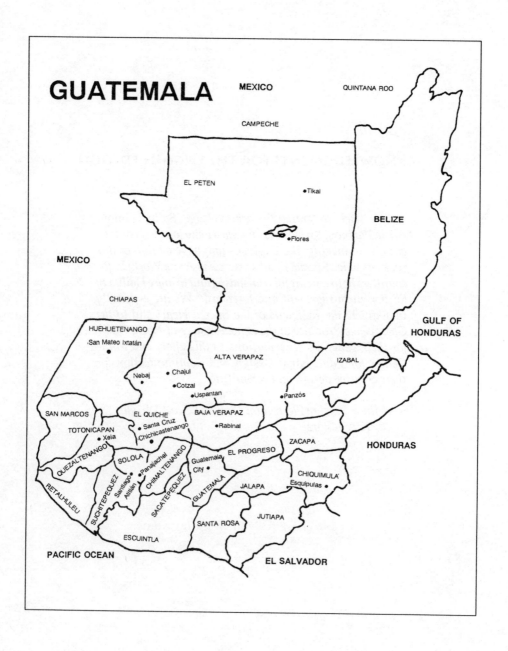

GUATEMALA

MEXICO

QUINTANA ROO

CAMPECHE

EL PETEN

•Tikal

BELIZE

MEXICO

•Flores

CHIAPAS

GULF OF
HONDURAS

HUEHUETENANGO

San Mateo Ixtatán •

ALTA VERAPAZ

IZABAL

Nebaj • •Chajul
•Cotzal
•Uspantan

•Panzós

SAN MARCOS

EL QUICHE

BAJA VERAPAZ

TOTONICAPAN
•Xela
•Santa Cruz
•Chichicastenango

•Rabinal

ZACAPA

QUEZALTENANGO

SOLOLA
Panajachel•
Santiago•
Atitlán

CHIMALTENANGO

Guatemala
City •

EL PROGRESO

HONDURAS

RETALHULEU

SUCHITEPEQUEZ

SACATEPEQUEZ

GUATEMALA

JALAPA

CHIQUIMULA
•Esquipulas •

SANTA ROSA

JUTIAPA

ESCUINTLA

PACIFIC OCEAN

EL SALVADOR

DEDICATION

I offer these pages to the women of Guatemala. These poems are simple plants born of our hard reality.

More than poems, they are deep breaths which allow me to keep going in the hope that life is more powerful than death. They express urgency and the hope that we do all we can to expand the space in which we can live together as human beings, respecting and defending life.

These words are for you, women of Guatemala---indigenous, girls, widows, old and young---wherever you are. Among the communities of resistance in the mountains or trying to survive in the cities. Living in villages occupied by the Army or living as refugees in Mexico, Belize, Honduras, Costa Rica, Nicaragua, Bolivia, the United States or Canada. Yours has been an experience so incredible that, because of all you have suffered and continue to suffer, it has pushed you to organize as the National Coordination of Guatemalan Widows - CONAVIGUA.

These poems are for you, working women that survive as domestics; for you, women who carry on your back baskets and bundles in the market; for you, homemakers who perform daily miracles to stretch pennies so that they last until the end of the month; for you, women who work in government offices; for you, women of the Mutual Support Group - GAM[1] whose lives are in danger every minute; for you, women who are teachers, union

members, laborers, *campesinas*, journalists, profession-
als, students, writers, nuns, Christians, Catholics and
Protestants, Jews, Adventists or of any other religious
faith.

   For you, women in exile; for you, mothers,
grandmothers, sisters who wait for the return of
your children or family members who have been
condemned to exile for daring to think and to say
what they think.

   These pages are also dedicated to you,
women who have preferred to live a comfortable
life, concerning yourself only with yourself and your
small nuclear family ... and who, nonetheless, are
not happy...

   Finally, these pages are dedicated in a special
way to all of you, men and women, who, torn apart
by the terrible situation in which so many Guatema-
lans live, have let go little by little of all you clung to
and, with nothing left to hold on to, have felt free to
become brothers and sisters with all those whom we
have crucified: the illiterate, the anemic, the sick
who have no medical care, the unemployed and the
laid off, those who have been pushed into crime,
beggars, the persecuted... The list is very long.
Every day we find ourselves with them wherever we
are in Guatemala.

--Julia Esquivel

---

[1] The Mutual Support Group or *Grupo de Apoyo Mutuo - GAM* is an organization
of men and women whose family members have been disappeared or
assassinated.

contents

~

FOREWORD

...What won't let us sleep
what won't let us rest
what won't stop pulsing away
here within
is the silent warm weeping
of the Indian women without their husbands,
the tragic gaze of the children
engraved deep down in our memory....
            --from "We Dream Awake," by Julia Esquivel

I t was just a few months after the assassina-
tion of Archbishop Oscar Romero of El Salvador
that a friend pressed into my hand some poetry
by Julia Esquivel. I had felt the shock waves that
jolted the globe after Romero's death in March 1980,
and some of them penetrated my own soul. For the
first time, I understood the pain that engulfed Central
America.

What was often said then was that the
archbishop was only the most visible victim of the
repression that had a stranglehold on the region.
When I read the poetry of Julia Esquivel, I under-
stood. Her poems gave voice to all the anonymous
martyrs who otherwise would have died forgotten,
to all the "silent warm weeping" and the tragic
gazes. And they drew me more deeply into the
dramatic history that was unfolding in Central
America.

A few months later, when we at *Sojourners* magazine were deciding the focus of our December 1980 issue--keeping our annual tradition of making December an "incarnation" issue about someone who speaks to us of the life of Christ--we made an unusual choice. Rather than choosing an individual as we typically did, we chose to focus on the faithful in Central America. We included "We Dream Awake" in that issue.

Six gone just now...
and nine in Rabinal,
And two and two and two,
and ten and a hundred and a thousand...
a whole army
witness to our pain,
to our fear,
to our courage,
to our hope!

What became true for many of us North Americans during that time more than a decade ago was that we began to be inspired and converted by the faith of the people of Central America. They taught us about the connection between cross and resurrection; they offered a hope that defied all the odds.

And so when Julia Esquivel came to Washington, D.C., in early 1981, I couldn't pass up the opportunity to meet her. I invited her to my apartment for breakfast.

I knew that Julia had been the editor of the banned Guatemalan magazine *Dialogo*, had received several threats on her life, and was living in exile. My first impression was one of surprise that a woman so outspoken and courageous could be so small and humble.

We were both trying to do better with the other's language, so she spoke to me in English and I to her in Spanish, promising to correct one another's mistakes. As we talked, black smoke suddenly began pouring out of the toaster. I pulled out two pieces of bread, burnt to a char.

"Perfect!" exclaimed Julia with a smile that filled her face with beautiful wrinkles. "It's exactly the way I like it." I apologized, declaring that she didn't have to eat burnt toast just to make me feel better about my competence as a breakfast cook.

"No," she explained, "it is good for my throat." And just to prove it, she pulled out a small box filled with carbon tablets that she took for a bronchial condition.

I will never forget that morning. There was something so poignant about Julia's kindness and faith, about the fact that she had suffered so much in her life and could still make the most of a piece of burnt toast.

She talked about the ways her government was trying to silence her and her people. As a fellow journalist, she asked me to help be the voice of the people of Central America. I was humbled by her request.

In the decade since, I have traveled to Central America and been moved by the incredible hope I have seen there. I have tried in my own small way to be faithful to Julia's request, writing the stories of suffering and courage that deeply changed my life. I have tried to be a voice; and she has been my memory, never letting me forget the silent warm weeping and the tragic gazes.

What won't let us sleep
is that we've been threatened with Resurrection!
Because every evening,
tired by now from the endless
counting since 1954,
we still go on loving life
and we won't accept their death.

We've been threatened with Resurrection
because we've touched their lifeless bodies
and their souls have penetrated our own,
now doubly strengthened.

In Guatemala, since the 1954 CIA-sponsored coup that replaced democracy with a military dictator, the counting has not stopped. The blood-bath has not ended. But neither have the dreams.

As we celebrate El Salvador's fragile peace after a 12-year civil war, let us not forget that there is still work to be done--and prayers to be offered--for our sisters and brothers in Central America who still await the dawn. And let us remember again how much we need their hope as we work to change the policies of our own government that encourage the repression.

I thank Julia Esquivel for offering us sustenance for the task, for bringing into our lives the people who otherwise would live and die in anonymity, silently crucified by power and greed. May we never forget them and their hope. And may we make their dreams our own. As Julia writes,

Because in this Marathon of hope,
there are always replacements
to carry on the strength
until we reach that goal
beyond death....

Be with us in this vigil
and you'll learn what it means to dream
you'll know then
how wonderful it is
to live threatened with Resurrection!

To dream, awake
to watch, asleep
to live, dying
and to know yourself already
Risen!

--Joyce Hollyday
   Associate Editor of Sojourners magazine

INTRODUCTION

W hy is so little known of Guatemala's crucifixion?" pleads Julia Esquivel. During the 1980s, the darkest decade in the history of Guatemala since the Conquest, Julia traveled the major capitals of Western Europe and North America denouncing the repression which had made the Guatemalan military governments the worst human rights offenders in Latin America. She described to the international community in painful detail the successive atrocities committed by the military. She explained that in the 1960s Guatemala was the first country in Latin America to experience forced disappearances of opposition figures, that "model villages" were military concentration camps, and that the Army had remained the power behind the throne after the election of the Christian Democrats.

In those visits Julia always did two things. She lifted up the vision of a different Guatemala, a Guatemala which respected life, cultural diversity and pluralism and which offered dignity to the poor; it was the Guatemala of the decade of democracy from 1944-1954 before the U.S.-sponsored military coup; it was the Guatemala of an "eternal spring." Secondly, Julia would make a plea for action from her listeners to defend the lives of those being tortured, killed, trampled on. Reading the latest communique describing a massacre or a disappearance, Julia implored that we turn our eyes to the holocaust which was happening and do all that we could to halt it.

Why is so little known about Guatemala's crucifixion? This is in part because indigenous Guatemala has been, and remains, a colonized country. The official history is in the hands of the conquerors and the truth is divulged at great risk. This book represents a courageous attempt to divulge the truth, not so much by narrating facts and analysis, but by revealing the hope which refuses to die.

TIME OF VIOLENCE

Since the 1954 CIA-sponsored coup which overthrew the democratic government of Jacobo Arbenz, darkness has descended on Guatemala. Thirty years of military dictatorships, each one seemingly more brutal than its predecessor, followed the U.S. intervention. Col. Castillo Armas, who overthrew Arbenz, was assassinated in 1957 and the general who replaced him was overthrown in another coup in 1963. The U.S. sent the Green Berets in 1966 to put down a popular rebellion that numbered no more than 450 men and to devise a counterinsurgency campaign in which 7,000 people were killed by government paramilitary squads. Amnesty International cited 20,000 death squad killings from 1966 to 1976 under three different military regimes. The victims were peasants, trade unionists, priests, nuns, students, opposition figures- -anyone suspected of "subversive" activity. For Guatemalans, two events particularly symbolize this *tiempo de violencia*, of wanton killing by the military: the slaughter of over one hundred unarmed peasants who were protesting about a land dispute in Panzós on May 27, 1978 and the January 31, 1980 firebombing by police of the Spanish Embassy killing all 39 protestors inside, who were seeking refuge from the authorities.

Church organizing among the indigenous people in the highland region in the early 1970s gave the peasants reason to hope and the Army reason to fear. Motivated by an interpretation of the Gospel which committed the Church to the poor, many priests and nuns taught literacy, built clinics and schools, and organized the people into Catholic Action cooperatives in order to address the material and economic needs. Most importantly, their experience brought people to reflect on the desperate conditions of their lives and to struggle for new possibilities. Repression and desperation radicalized many of the lay pastoral workers who in 1977 formed the Committee for Peasant Unity (CUC) to organize peasants to protest social, political and economic injustices.

The seeds of guerrilla insurgency which had been present since 1962 began to grow, particularly in the highlands, where the living conditions were most desperate and the church-promoted *conscienticization* work (the process of raising the awareness of the marginalized people) was most advanced. Though the guerrillas were never able to make a serious attempt to take power, the military governments of Gen. Lucas García (1978-1982) and Gen. Ríos Montt (1982-1983) launched a murderous counterinsurgency campaign committing hundreds of brutal massacres in indigenous communities. Four hundred and forty-one villages were completely destroyed and all of their inhabitants either hunted down or forced to flee. Ríos Montt, an evangelical who claimed he had been personally chosen by God to lead Guatemala, executed by firing squad hundreds of opponents of the regime. Government sponsored death squads killed randomly and with absolute impunity.

Church people, like other sectors of society, were caught in the violence. Fifteen priests and hundreds of catechists were assassinated forcing the Diocese of Quiché to close and its bishop, Juan Gerardi, into political exile. Church leaders formed the Pro Justice and Peace Committee to denounce the repression internationally. Julia herself was abducted off the streets of Guatemala City by the security forces and after intense international pressure on the government she was released alive. She left to go into exile in 1980.

Over one hundred thousand people have been murdered in the counterinsurgency campaign, and hundreds of thousands more have been displaced internally or forced to flee the country. The people of Guatemala have been living through, according to Jesuit priest Ricardo Falla, "the dark night, a sense of impotence and destitution experienced at the deepest level."

THE CONQUEST

Since 1524, conquest and resistance have been in contention in Guatemala. When the Spanish conquistador Pedro de Alvarado first invaded Guatemala, the Quiché prince Tecún Umán led ten thousand Quiché warriors against the invaders on the banks of what is now the Olintepeque river in southern Guatemala. They were annihilated by the Spaniards' artillery, and the water was turned red by the flowing blood of Tecún Umán and his men so that the river became known as "Xequijel," meaning "under blood." During the battle, a quetzal bird, with its long beautiful tail, was struck in the chest by Spanish fire and succumbed, gaining its reputation for being unable to live in captivity.

In recent decades the commemoration of the uprising of Tecún Umán has been an official act presided over by Guatemala's generals. This past year on February 20, 1992, four generals led a ceremony at Liberty Plaza in Guatemala City to honor the "soldiers of the Fatherland who are in the mountains defending our liberty and opposing foreign doctrines." The indigenous majority of Guatemala has always rejected the celebration as another aspect of military propaganda which serves to hide the truth. However, this year on the same day as the official ceremony, hundreds of indigenous people gathered on the banks of the Olintepeque river for the first time to publicly commemorate and reclaim the memory of Tecún Umán and his men who "instead of submitting, resisted; instead of surrendering, fought." During the alternative ceremony, one indigenous leader declared, "From 1524 until the present we have engaged in one long struggle. Patzicía (1944), Sansirisay (1974), Panzós (1978), Santiago Atitlán (1990) [sites of indigenous resistance]."

Third grade Guatemalan textbooks, distributed by the U.S. Agency for International Development (AID), characterize the indigenous population as "grateful to serve" their Spanish conquerors. The textbook history somehow does not account for the fate of the estimated twelve million Indians in the region who died from violence or disease in the first hundred years of Spanish rule nor does it recognize major Indian revolts which occurred at least every generation against the Spanish and their policies of genocide and slavery. Revolts such as the 1633 uprisings in Verapaz, the 1708 rebellion in Chiapas (then part of Guatemala), the 1748 Mam revolt in Ixtahuacán, the 1764 Cakchiquel uprising in Tecpán and numerous others. In 1820 the year before Central America gained independence from Spain, Atanasio Tzul led a successful Quiché revolt in Totonicapán. Once in power, he ended forced tribute and wrote a new constitution before being deposed by Spanish troops. Though the indigenous never gained military superiority, their will to resist was never crushed.

Independence for Guatemala did not change the conditions of virtual economic slavery for the indigenous people. Indigenous people traditionally farmed and owned the land, almost all of it without legal title, in a communal manner. As coffee gained value in international markets, the government perpetrated a legal theft of land owned by the indigenous. In 1884 alone, 100,000 acres of land was taken from the indigenous and passed into the hands of large plantation owners. Guatemala developed a feudal economy in which vagrancy laws requiring Indian men to work 150 days with minimal or no wages ensured an ample supply of laborers during the peak harvest seasons of coffee, sugar cane, cotton and bananas.

THE DECADE OF DEMOCRACY

In 1944, the dictator Jorge Ubico was overthrown, giving birth to Guatemala's only experiment with democracy since the Spanish invasion. Juan José Arévalo, who believed in "spiri-

tual socialism," was elected by popular vote and
began cautiously to implement reforms. A new
constitution was written enfranchising for the first
time illiterate males and literate females over the age
of 18. Arévalo built rural clinics and schools and
passed social security legislation. He abolished the
hated vagrancy law and legalized farmworker unions
on plantations which employed more than 500
workers. The oligarchy and military abhorred the
new reforms but the animosity that could have led to
a military coup was defused in part by the election of
a former military colonel, Jacobo Arbenz, to succeed
Arévalo.

      Arbenz believed that capital had a social
function and that the poor had to be integrated into a
market economy. That could only be done by giving
the landless access to land in a country which had
(and has) the most unequal land distribution in Latin
America. Two thirds of the arable land continues to
be held by 2% of the population. The 1952 Agrarian
Reform Law passed by Arbenz empowered the
government to purchase unused land owned by large
landowners. When the government expropriated
with compensation 372,000 acres owned by United
Fruit Company to distribute among 23,000 peasants,
the government lit a powderkeg. John Foster Dulles,
U.S. Secretary of State and a major stockholder of
United Fruit, and his brother, Alan Dulles, Director
of the Central Intelligence Agency (CIA), moved
quickly to provide mercenaries, air cover and inter-
national support to a little-known colonel to success-
fully overthrow Arbenz. The ten years of spring had
come to an end.

THE LEGACY OF CONQUEST

In 1984 with the economy faltering and
their international standing at pariah status, the
military in Guatemala finally bowed to international
pressure to allow a civilian government. The Chris-
tian Democrat party, under Vinicio Cerezo, won the
1985 elections raising expectations of an economic
turnaround and an end to the abuses. Two years
later however, the economic situation had deterio-
rated further and accusations of corruption against
Cerezo and his inner circle were widespread. On the
street, people joked that the Christian Democrats
were neither "Christian" nor "democrats." Few
people, however, made light of the human rights
situation which continued to be appalling.

Under civilian rule, the military continued to
commit massacres (Aguacayo, Santiago Atitlán),
political assassinations (304 in 1990 alone according
to the Guatemalan Congress) and forced disappear-
ances (223 reported cases during the same year).
Human rights observers allege that Cerezo's own
personal security guard brutally assassinated Myrna
Mack, a Guatemalan anthropologist who was investi-
gating the situation of the displaced. Even the U.S.
State Department, not known for its enlightened
human rights policy towards Guatemala over the past
decade, was forced to reconsider its position. After
the decapitation of a U.S. businessman and the rape
and torture of a U.S. nun, the U.S. suspended mili-
tary aid to the Guatemalan government in 1990.

The 1990 election of a fundamentalist
Protestant, Jorge Elías Serrano, as president has
produced few changes. From January 1, 1991 until
February 13, 1992 the Guatemalan Human Rights

Commission reported 896 extrajudicial executions. In economic terms, the life of the poor is dire: 76% of the children are malnourished; 89% of the population lives in poverty and 67% live in absolute poverty according to U.N. figures. Not surprisingly, the situation is worse for indigenous people than it is for *ladinos* (people of mixed indigenous and European heritage). Social indicators for education, for example, reveal that 62.7% of the indigenous are illiterate compared to 37% of the *ladinos*. In the capital, the government spends about 28 *quetzales* (about $5.30) per habitant while in the indigenous communities the government spends 2.50 *quetzales* (about $0.50)

The past five centuries of conquest and in particular the past forty years of military dictatorships and corrupt civilian governments have produced a shocking legacy of death. For the indigenous, Guatemala is no less colonized now than it was four centuries ago. The $1.50 per day wages during harvests today are slave wages; the conditions on the plantations on the coast are little better than the conditions in the gold and silver mines centuries earlier. Whether ruled by the Spanish conquistadors, the *criollos*, the U.S.-funded mercenaries, the generals, or civilians wearing a presidential sash, the indigenous are faced with policies designed to exploit, disempower and de-humanize them. Mayan parents today say the same thing Mayan parents said four centuries ago: "Our children are born to die."

THE CERTAINTY OF SPRING

Where is the hope in Guatemala? Where is the spring after what Julia Esquivel calls the "thou-

sand years of death?'' While the darkness has not
lifted, signs of hope persist in the communities, in
popular organizations, and in the churches. Guate-
mala has one of the largest populations of indigenous
people of any country in Latin America. In spite of
persecution---even genocide---they have survived
and their culture has endured. Indications are that,
in a number of important ways, they are claiming
more assertively their cultural distinctness which is a
tremendous sign of hope. The indigenous celebra-
tion of the anniversary of the uprising of Tecún
Umán is a just one example.

Hope also springs from the participation of
the poor, particularly the indigenous poor, in the re-
emergence of the popular movement. On October
12, 1991 fifty thousand mainly indigenous people
marched in Quezaltenango in support of the Conti-
nental Campaign of Popular, Indigenous and Black
Resistance which reflects the re-kindling of
grassroots organizing that is happening throughout
the country. The other light piercing the darkness is
the resurgence of Christian base communities which
had ceased to function due to the repression. They
are meeting again, some clandestinely, some openly.
Out of the people's experience of persecution has
come a profound theology which affirms life. Their
theology of life is rooted in the harsh realities of
poverty and repression, in traditional Mayan beliefs
and in scriptural reflection. Julia writes elsewhere,

> Five hundred years of oppression have not diminished our
> faith in our Creator. We bear witness in our struggles
> and in our hope to our faith in a God of life who is also
> the God of the poor... The struggle for justice opens our
> eyes so that we recognize the creation for what it is: our
> home and the home of all people, the source of life.

--Editors
The Ecumenical Program on Central America and the Caribbean

ALL
GUATEMALA

~

CERTEZA

"Podrán cortar todas las flores
pero siempre volverá la Primavera".
Florecerás Guatemala.

Cada gota de sangre,
cada lágrima,
cada sollozo apagado por las balas,
cada grito de horror,
cada pedazo de piel
arrancado por el odio
de los anti-hombres,
florecerán.

El sudor que brotaba
de nuestra angustia
huyendo de la policía,
y el suspiro escondido
en lo más secreto de nuestro miedo
florecerán.

Hemos vivido mil años de muerte
en una Patria
que será toda
"Una eterna Primavera".

Bommersvik
Agosto 20 de 1983

CERTAINTY

"They can cut all the flowers
But Spring will always return."
Guatemala you will bloom.

Every drop of blood,
every tear,
every sob extinguished by bullets,
every cry of horror,
every shred of skin
torn away in hatred
by the anti-humans--
will bloom.

The sweat that broke out
of our anguish
fleeing from the police
and the sigh concealed
in the most secret of our fears--
will bloom.

We have lived a thousand years of death
in a Homeland
that will be altogether
"An eternal Spring."

                              Bommersvik
                         August 20, 1983

¿POR QUE?

¿Por qué de la crucifixión
de Guatemala
se sabe tan poco?

¿Por qué las delegaciones
y los periódicos
y la gente importante
se ocupan gustosos
de Argentina y de Chile
de Haití y de Filipinas
de El Salvador y de Honduras?

¿Por qué no de Guatemala?

Sabes amiga,
nuestra pequeña
Guatemala herida
Tierra de viudas y huérfanos...
Nuestra patria hermana,
es sólo una mujer.
¿Comprendes ahora?

Ginebra, Suiza
Marzo 19 de 1986

WHY?

Why is so little known
of Guatemala's
crucifixion?

Why do the delegations
and the newspapers
and the important people
worry zealously
over Argentina and Chile,
over Haiti and the Philippines
over El Salvador and Honduras?

Why not over Guatemala?

You know, my friend,
our little wounded
Guatemala
Land of widows and orphans,
our sister homeland
is only a woman.
Now do you understand?

Geneva, Switzerland
March 19, 1986

SALARIO

Tan cerca de tí, Guatemala,
y tan lejos,
tan próxima y tan lejana.
Fundida, metida en mí
como mi corazón, o mis lágrimas,
o mis pupilas
impregnadas de tu paisaje
inigualable,
y tan lejos...

Porque si aprovechando
este momento
me metiera adentro
de tu geografía inconfundible,
estaría alejándome
como nunca antes,
de tu futuro abierto
a la libertad verdadera.
Porque si cediendo
a lo que añoran mis ojos,
y mis manos
y mis raíces más profundas,
me dejara atrapar
por el presente aparente
perdería para siempre
tu futuro luminoso.

Tan cerca de tí, Guatemala,
y tan lejos!

Nueva Nicaragua
Enero 15 de 1987

A LIVING WAGE

So close to you, Guatemala,
and yet so far away,
so near and yet so distant.
Rooted, infused in me
like my heart or my tears,
or my pupils
impregnated with your incomparable
landscape
and so far away ...
Because if
seizing this moment
I were to immerse myself right into your
unmistakable geography,
I would be moving further away
than ever
from your future
open to freedom.

Because if
yielding to the longing of my eyes
and my hands
and my deepest roots
I allowed the apparent present
to trap me
I would lose your shining future
forever.

So close to you, Guatemala,
and yet so far away!

Nicaragua
January 15, 1987

TODA GUATEMALA

Toda Guatemala es una Rigoberta Menchú.

Nos han matado a nuestros padres,
a unos, con los trabajos forzados
pagados con miseria y enfermedades.
A otros, venadeados los días de fiesta
por negarse a hacer el servicio militar
"obligatorio" para los indios,
y a otros, en el parque de Panzós
o en una cooperativa del Ixcán
bajo la macabra apertura democrática
de Kjell Eugenio Laugerud García.

La guerra de exterminio del general Lucas
se tragó a muchos otros en los cementerios
          clandestinos,
en los barrancos y en las aldeas arrasadas.
Y ahora, los que nos quedan todavía
que andan huyendo por los montes,
por las cuevas y los barrancos
de las grandes matazones e incendios
realizados por los soldados, son perseguidos
por el "nuevo ejército" del presidente evangelista
para castrarlos de la verdad por la fuerza
como lo hicieron con el "cuache" Pellecer
para convertirlos en asesinos de sus hermanos
bien controlados en las aldeas modelo
en donde tendrán pan con mentira,
financiados por los fundamentalistas
del verbo y de los comunitarianistas
de los Estados Unidos, hermanos espirituales
del general Efraín Ríos Montt.

ALL GUATEMALA

All Guatemala is a Rigoberta Menchú.[1]

They have killed our parents--
some by forced labor,
wages of misery and disease.
Others hunted down like deer on fiesta days
for refusing military service
"obligatory" for Indians,
and others killed in the plaza at Panzós[2]
or in a cooperative in the Ixcan[3]
during the horror-filled "democratic opening"
under Kjell Eugenio Laugerud Garcia.[4]

General Lucas'[5] war of extermination
swallowed up many more in clandestine cemeteries,
in ravines and in decimated villages.
And now, those who still remain,
who live on the run in the mountains,
in caves and ravines,
fleeing the slaughter and the burning
brought by the soldiers--they are persecuted
by this "new army" of the president-evangelist
who by force would castrate the truth from them
as they did to Luis Pellecer,[6]
turning them into their brothers' assassins
carefully controlled in model villages
where they will break bread with lies,
paid for by fundamentalists of the Church of the Word
and by evangelicals
from the United States, spiritual brothers
of General Efraín Ríos Montt.[7]

Toda Guatemala es una Rigoberta Menchú.

Violaron a nuestra madre tierra
cuando pelaron la costa sur
y cambiaron el equilibro ecológico
sembrando algodón para producir capital,
en vez de sembrar el santo maíz de cada día
para mantener la vida el pueblo.
Violaron a nuestra madre tierra
cuando envenenaron los ríos y mataron los peces
y los raquíticos animalitos de los parcelarios
de la "ESPERANZA," como mataron a su pastor,
--don Santos Jiménez Martínez--
Violaron a nuestra madre,
cuando violaron a tu madre, Rigoberta...
y la dejaron morir lentamente, torturada
bajo un arbol como trampa,
para hacerte caer a tí y a tus hermanas.
Le abrieron el vientre a la tierra
y a la vida...
como se lo abren a las indias embarazadas
para sacarles al niño y sembrarles la muerte.

Toda Guatemala es una Rigoberta Menchú.

Han quemado vivos a nuestros hermanos
bajo el sol ardiente de las algodoneras
llenándoles los pulmones de gamezán.
Millares se fueron acabando
como candelitas de sebo
o como milpitas sin agua...
Otros, retorcidos bajo el fósforo
en la embajada de España.

All Guatemala is a Rigoberta Menchú.

They raped our mother earth
when they stripped the southern coast
and changed the ecological balance
planting cotton to produce capital
instead of sacred corn,
which sustains our people.
They raped our mother earth
when they poisoned the rivers and killed the fish
and the rickety little creatures on plots of land
of a cooperative called "Hope"
as they killed the pastor, Don Santos Jiménez
        Martínez.
They raped our mother,
when they raped your mother, Rigoberta ...
when they left her, tortured, to die slowly
under a tree, as a trap
to bring you down, too, you and your sisters.
They ripped open the womb of the earth
and of life ...
the way they rip open pregnant Indian women
to tear out the child and sow death within.

All Guatemala is a Rigoberta Menchú.

They've burned our sisters and brothers alive
under the blistering sun of the cottonfields,
filling their lungs with pesticides.
Thousands have perished, snuffed out
like little tallow candles
or fields without water ...
others, writhing in the flames
in the Spanish Embassy.[8]

---

[1] Rigoberta Menchú is a Guatemalan indigenous leader with the
Committee of Peasant Unity (CUC). Rigoberta has lived in exile since the
early 1980s.

[2] Government troops massacred over 100 Kekchi people on May 29,
1978 in the plaza of Panzós, Alta Verapaz. The campesinos were protesting
land evictions.

Otros, bajo el napalm o la metralla
regados por los helicópteros artillados
donados por el gobierno "democrático"
de Ronald Reagan y de Alexander Haig,
o bajo la descarga mortal de los aviones Pilatus
artillados en Bruselas.
Otros, hinchados como vejigas de Corpus Christi,
cuyos cuerpos, bañados en gasolina,
revivieron el infierno de Nerón
en la plaza de Chajul,
como nuestro hermanito Patrocinio,
el catequista, Rigoberta.

Toda Guatemala es una Rigoberta Menchú.

Vamos con ella, por el mundo civilizado,
clamando a Dios, contándole a sus hijos
que queremos vivir,
que ya no podemos aguantar
el macabro amor de Ríos Montt
que tortura, deguella, quema y extermina
a nuestros abuelos, a nuestra madre y a nuestros
                niños
y transforma todo el altiplano en un Vietnam
                infernal.

Toda Guatemala es una Rigoberta Menchú.

¿Qué esperan los cristianos del mundo "libre"
para apagar esta hoguera encendida
por los hijos del "monte Diablo" en Guatemala?

Others, by napalm or machine guns,
strafed by armored helicopters
donated by the "democratic" government
of Ronald Reagan and Alexander Haig,
or beneath the deadly payload of Pilatus airplanes
outfitted in Brussels.
Others, swollen like the balloons of Corpus Christi,
their bodies soaked in gasoline,
relived the hell of Nero
in the plaza of Chajul,[9]
like our little brother Patrocinio[10] the catechist,
         Rigoberta.

All Guatemala is a Rigoberta Menchú.

We go with her, throughout the civilized world,
crying out to God, telling God's children
that we want to live,
that we can't stand another day
of the horrid love of Ríos Montt,
which tortures, decapitates, burns and exterminates
our grandparents, our mother, our children
and turns the mountains into an infernal Vietnam.

All Guatemala is a Rigoberta Menchú.

What are they waiting for, those "free world"
         Christians?
When will they put out the fire
lit in Guatemala by the sons of Mt. Diablo?[11]

---

[3] The Ixcán is a jungle region in the northern part of the Department of
Quiché where Catholic Action land cooperatives were established in the
1970s. Military repression targetted the cooperatives and destroyed the
communities.

[4] General Kjell Eugenio Laugerud García became president in 1974
through a rigged election.

[5] General Fernando Romeo Lucas García won the presidency in March,
1978 as a result of a fraudulent election and was responsible for the

Toda Guatemala es una Rigoberta Menchú.

Hermana, hermano: no queremos el exterminio
de nuestros padres ni de nuestros hermanos
como ocurrió con millones en la segunda guerra,
la guerra sin sentido de los blancos,
o como ocurre en las películas del oeste
contra los indios dominados en lo que
ahora se llaman, "los Estados Unidos..."
No queremos que continúe el suplicio
de nuestro pueblo indio,
Presentimos...si así ocurriera,
que sepultaríamos toda esperanza de Vida
para toda la familia humana:
UNA SOLA SOBRE TODA LA TIERRA!

Toda Guatemala es una Rigoberta Menchú.

1983

All Guatemala is a Rigoberta Menchú.

My sister, my brother: we do not want the
            extermination
of our parents and our siblings,
as happened to millions in World War Two,
(the senseless war of the whites),
or to defeated Indians in "Westerns"
in what is now called "the United States..."
We do not want the anguish to continue
for our Indian people,
and we fear that, should this happen,
we would bury all hope of Life,
for the entire human family:
ONE FAMILY ON THE FACE OF THE EARTH!

All Guatemala is a Rigoberta Menchú.

                                        1983

_____

deaths of thousands of innocent civilians during his rule from 1978-
1982.

[6] Fr. Luis Pellecer was a Jesuit priest who was kidnapped in September
1981 by Guatemalan security forces. After being subjected to
brainwashing, he read a "confession" on national television linking
Church activities with the guerrilla insurgency.

[7] General Efraín Ríos Montt took power in March, 1982 through a
military coup. He launched a counter-insurgency campaign known as
"beans and guns" which killed thousands of indigenous campesinos in the
Guatemalan highlands.

[8] On January 31, 1980 CUC members took refuge in the Spanish
Embassy after their non-violent march was repressed. The Guatemalan
police forces then stormed the Embassy, killing all 39 occupants inside,
including Vicente Menchú, the father of Rigoberta Menchú.

[9] In 1981 the Guatemalan Army launched a series of attacks on Chajul,
bombing the convent and killing more than 35 people.

[10] Patrocinio Menchú, a brother of Rigoberta, was executed by
Guatemalan security forces.

[11] A reference to the construction of the California-based Mt. Diablo
nuclear plant which sparked citizens' protests.

TIERRA SANTA

Belem no está lejos, hermano
está allí en "El Adelanto", en Pujujil
donde un niñito de nueve meses murió indefenso
con un pedazo del pecho de su madre entre su boquita
        sedienta,
cuando el Ejército de la Junta Militar
macheteó a su madre y partió en pedazos su carne tierna
para después prenderle fuego
como en tiempos de Herodes y Nerón.

Nazareth no está lejos, hermana.
Está allí donde Pedrito, el niño indio
dejó el azadón y tomó el machete
para defender la virginidad de su hermana
y la dignidad de su abuela y de su madre
cuando los soldados vestidos de paisanos
llegaron a sembrar el terror y la muerte.

En el camino a Jericó que está entre El Salvador y
        Guatemala
los salteadores y bandidos están despojando a Jesús
de su túnica de colores, huipil de mi pueblo,
trapo santo, manchado de sangre inocente.
Escupen su cara, lo castran y torturan
mientras los falsos pastores no tienen tiempo de defenderlo
porque van a sus negocios o a sus templos
ascépticos de amor y de humanidad.

Betania está a la vuelta de Chajul.
Allí donde un oficial entrenado en la zona del Canal
ordenó que quemaran vivo a Patrocinio Menchú
y al cuarto día su espíritu levantó mil en la montaña.

HOLY LAND

Bethlehem is not far from here, my brother.
It is right there in "El Adelanto,"[1] in Pujujil
where a nine-month-old infant died helplessly
with a bit of his mother's breast in his dry mouth
when the Army of the military junta
hacked his mother with a machete and tore her
          tender flesh,
then burnt her, as in the days of Herod and Nero.

Nazareth is not far from here, my sister.
It is right there where Pedrito the Indian boy
put down his hoe and picked up a machete
to defend his sister's virginity
and his mother's and grandmother's dignity
when soldiers dressed in civilian clothes
arrived to spread terror and death.

On the road to Jericho that lies between El
          Salvador and Guatemala
the assailants and robbers are mugging Jesus,
stripping him of his multicolored tunic, the *huipil* of
          my people,
sacred rag, stained with innocent blood.
They spit in his face, they castrate and torture him
while the false pastors have no time to defend him
because they're on business or at church,
in places washed clean of love and humanity.

Bethany lies on the other side of Chajul.
Right there, where an officer trained in the Canal
          Zone[2]
ordered death by burning for Patrocinio Menchú
and on the fourth day his spirit raised a thousand in
          the mountains.

Si pasas por Samaria, allí nada más,
junto a la segunda pila del Incienso,
busca a la que tenía que vender su cuerpo
para darle de comer a sus hijos
drogadictos y antisociales ya a los 7 años,
los mismos que me evangelizaron a mí,
los que me mostraron cuán superficial
y abstracto era eso que nosotros, los evangélicos,
llamábamos "amor cristiano".

¿Y el Calvario? Está al norte de Chupol.
Allí mismo en donde los aviones volando en círculos
acribillaron a ancianos, niños y mujeres indios.
Allí donde las madres lloraron a gritos
la pérdida de sus niños pequeñitos.
Allí en donde Raquel no quiso ser consolada,
cuando los soldados de Herodes
degollaron o machetearon a sus hijos.

Si no reconoces Belem, o Nazareth o Betania.
Si te resistes a subir con el pueblo al Calvario,
tus ojos ciegos no podrán reconocer al Resucitado
en el Huerto de los Aromas que será Guatemala
cuando la fuerza de la VIDA rompa el sello imperial
y se abra Nuestra Historia a la Nueva Alborada!

Berlín
Mayo 25 de 1982

If you pass through Samaria, right over there,
next to the second well in Incienso,
seek out the one who had to sell her body
so as to feed her children
drug addicts and delinquents by the age of seven,
the same ones who evangelized me,
who showed me how superficial,
how abstract was that which we Evangelicals
used to call "Christian love."

And Calvary? It lies north of Chupol.
Right there where the circling planes
riddled the elderly with bullets, and the children,
and the Indian women.
Right there where the mothers wept and wailed
for the loss of their little children.
Right there where Rachel would not be consoled,
when Herod's soldiers
struck her children with machetes or slit their
            throats.

If you do not recognize Bethlehem, or Nazareth, or
            Bethany.
If you will not climb with the people to Calvary,
your blind eyes will not recognize the Resurrected
            One
in the Scented Garden that will be Guatemala
when the force of LIFE breaks the imperial seal
and opens Our History to a New Dawn!

                                        Berlin
                              May 25, 1982

---

[1] In El Adelanto, Solola, ten women were kidnapped and killed by 250
members of the security forces in April 1982. Incienso is a marginalized
community on the periphery of Guatemala City. Chajul and Chupol,
both of El Quiché, were sites of massacres.

[2] The Canal Zone refers to the U.S. military zone in Panama.

ELECCION

Me quedo con mi pueblo,
el despojado,
el engañado,
el perseguido,
el negociado.
Ese, que nunca ha sido considerado como humano
pero que se yergue siempre
y sobrevive,
y vuelve a empezar...

Me quedo con aquellos
que tres veces fueron despojados
y sacados de su tierra.
Los perseguidos como venados
por los montes y las selvas.

Me quedo con el pueblo silencioso...
que guarda en lo más íntimo
la palabra postrera.
Me quedo con los viejos,
con las viudas
y los huérfanos.

En el corazón quebrantado
de los débiles
Dios encuentra Su Fortaleza.

Sí, me quedo con mi Pueblo!

Octubre de 1984

THE CHOICE

I will remain with my people
the dispossessed
the deceived
the persecuted
the bargained-for.
With the people who have never been considered
              human
but who keep standing up
and surviving
and beginning again ...

I will remain with the ones
who have been three times dispossessed,
forced off their land.
The ones who've been chased like deer
through forests and jungles.

I will remain with the silent people ...
who guard in the intimacy of their hearts
the last word.
I remain with the elderly,
with the widows
and the orphans.

In the crushed hearts
of the weak
God finds Strength.

Yes, I will remain with my people!

October 1984

SUSPIRO

Cuando se tiene que beber tanto dolor
Cuando un río de angustia
ahoga nuestra respiración,
Cuando se ha llorado mucho
y las lágrimas brotan como ríos
de nuestros ojos tristes,
sólo entonces
el suspiro recóndito del prójimo,
es nuestro propio suspiro!

1985

THE SIGH

When it is necessary to drink so much pain,
when a river of anguish
drowns us,
when we have wept many tears
and they flow like rivers
from our sad eyes,
only then
does the deep hidden sigh of our neighbor
become our own.

1985

GUATEMALA TAMBIEN ES NICARAGUA

Guatemala también es Nicaragua,
hermano Nica.
También allí la CIA
sembró a la contra hace 32 años,
y un Reagan
que entonces se llamaba Eisenhower,
se metió en Honduras
para derrocar al "peligro comunista"
cuando el mundo aún no había aprendido
a pronunciar la palabra solidaridad...

Entonces,
Guatemala estuvo sola
frente a Goliath.

Hoy, más de veinte Somozas
devoran la carne
de los guatemaltecos pobres.

Sí hermano,
Guatemala también es Nicaragua.

Allí los contras han construido
muchas fronteras internas
y el dolor de 442 aldeas mártires
se viste de dignidad
en los campos de Chiapas,
en San Cristóbal,
Campeche y Quintana Roo,
que también son Guatemala...

GUATEMALA, TOO, IS NICARAGUA

Guatemala, too, is Nicaragua,
my Nicaraguan brother.
There, too, the CIA
planted the contras 32 years ago
and a Reagan
who then was named Eisenhower
moved into Honduras
to overthrow the "communist threat" in Guatemala[1]
when the world had not yet even learned
to say the word solidarity ...

In those days,
Guatemala stood alone
before Goliath.

Now, more than twenty Somozas
devour the flesh
of poor Guatemalans.

Yes, my brother,
Guatemala, too, is Nicaragua.

There the contras have established
internal military zones
and the sorrow of 442 martyred villages
is clothed in dignity
in the camps of Chiapas,
San Cristobal,
Campeche and Quintana Roo,[2]
which also are Guatemala ...

Por eso los Somozas
de Guatemala,
quieren vestirse de corderos
con la cara de Vinicio Cerezo
y con los discursos
de los "intelectuales apolíticos."[1]

Sí, hermano Nica,
recuérdalo,
compréndelo,
másticalo bien
en tu consciencia sandinista
y en tu corazón solidario:
Guatemala, también es Nicaragua.

Porque Guatemala, hermano,
es una chavala campesina
enflaquecida por la deuda externa
perseguida, violada y torturada
por los contras
entrenados con la plata de Bonn
y de Washington
y armados con galiles de Israel.

La "neutralidad activa"
es la carnada oportuna
para pescar bien
"la ayuda para el desarrollo"
que utilizarían los contras
para encadenar a 6 millones de pobres
que también son Nicaragua.

Por eso, hermano Nica,
para que nuestra patria
sea libre de verdad,
miles de muchachos y muchachas
siembran en las montañas
en las selvas
y en los valles,

And so the Somozas
of Guatemala
dress in sheep's clothing
with the face of Vinicio Cerezo[3]
and with the discourse
of the "apolitical intellectuals."[4]

Yes, my Nicaraguan brothers,
remember this,
understand this,
digest it well
in your Sandinista consciousness
and in your heart full of solidarity:
Guatemala, too, is Nicaragua.

Because Guatemala, my brother,
is a peasant girl
emaciated by foreign debt
persecuted, raped and tortured
by the contras
trained with money from Bonn
and from Washington
and armed with assault rifles from Israel.[5]

"Active neutrality" is
the perfect bait
for catching
"development aid"
that the contras will use
to chain down 6 million poor
who also are Nicaragua.

And so, my Nicaraguan brother,
so that our land
might be truly free,
thousands of young men and women
are in the mountains,
in the jungles
in the valleys,

la semilla de la justicia y del amor
que librará un día a su patria,
Guatemala.

Porque allí
en Guatemala,
el pobre que todavía gime
bajo el yugo de los Somozas
y lucha por la vida digna y libre
que tú ya empiezas a gustar,
también es Nicaragua.

Nueva Nicaragua
Enero de 1987

---

[1] Título de un poema del poeta guatemalteco Otto René Castillo.

planting the seeds of justice and love
that will one day free their country,
Guatemala.

For there,
in Guatemala,
the poor who still groan
under the yoke of the Somozas
and struggle for the freedom and dignity
that you have begun to taste,
they, too, are Nicaragua.

Nicaragua
January 1987

---

[1] In 1954 the U.S. sponsored a military coup against the democratically
elected Arbenz government employing mercenary troops that had been
based in neighboring Honduras.

[2] Chiapas, San Cristobal, Campeche and Quintana Roo are areas in
southern Mexico where 46,000 Guatemalan refugees reside.

[3] Vinicio Cerezo, a Christian Democrat and President of Guatemala from
1986-1990, was the first freely-elected civilian president in more than
thirty years. Cerezo ended his term under a storm of criticism and
accusation of involvement in corruption and human rights violations.

[4] Title of a poem by Guatemalan poet Otto Rene Castillo. Footnote in
original.

[5] The Israeli government acted as a conduit for military assistance to
Guatemala after the Carter Administration officially suspended U.S.
military assistance to Guatemala.

ORACION

No nos dejes caer en la tentación
y enséñanos a perdonar
como tú nos has perdonado.

Ten misericordia de los anti-hombres...
de los que como Caín,
aborrecen a su hermano
porque presienten que ante Tí
no hay acepción de personas
y tienen miedo...

Quisieran convertir al prójimo
en siervo,
y su mirada de hombre libre
los aterra y los empuja a aniquilarlo.

Ten misericordia de los que
como el rico,
se rellenan el vientre
con viandas escogidas
y vinos deliciosos,
mientras en sus fincas
sus mozos, como Lázaro,
desean el alimento de sus perros.
Campesinos-colonos, que para engañar
el hambre, comen una vez al día
durante cuatro o cinco meses al año...
y engendran hijos para la muerte...

Tú, Padre de Misericordia,
Dios profundamente humano,
que conoces la hondura de

PRAYER

Lead us not into temptation,
and teach us to forgive
as you have forgiven us.

Have mercy on the anti-humans ...
on those who, like Cain,
hate their brother
because they suspect that before you
there are no favorites
and they are afraid ...

They would like to make their neighbor
into a servant;
his free man's gaze
terrifies them, impels them to annihilate him.

Have mercy on those who,
like the rich,
fill up their bellies
with choice meats
and delicious wines,
while in their fields
their hired men, like Lazarus,
hunger for the food given to dogs.
Peasant-laborers who eat once a day
to fool their stomachs,
during four or five months of the year ...
and produce children only for death ...

Yes, Father of Mercy,
profoundly human God,
you who know the depths

nuestro sufrimiento,
provee de entrañas de misericordia
siquiera a uno de los generales
de mi país,
talvez un día sea posible
que ese ser
ya convertido en hombre,
moje su dedo en agua
para refrescar el fuego devorador
que consumirá todo el ser
de los poderosos de la tierra...

Provéenos a nosotros,
tus hijos, de esas entrañas tuyas,
porque, perdonar, Señor,
significa, amar de tal manera
que obliguemos a los hijos de Caín
a ser realmente tus hijos!

Háznos de verdad tus hijos, Señor!

Suiza
Marzo de 1985

of our suffering,
give a merciful heart
to just one of the generals
of my country
and perhaps one day
this being,
now turned human,
will dip his finger in water
to dampen the voracious fire
that will consume
all the powerful of the earth ...

Give to us, your children,
your own merciful heart
because forgiveness, my Lord,
means loving in such a way
that we oblige the sons of Cain
to be, in truth, your children!

Make us truly your children, Lord!

Switzerland
March 1985

PADRE, TU CORAZON HERIDO

Yo conozco tu corazón herido, Padre.
Te he oído gemir, como al viejo Job,
he escuchado tus sollozos
y he sentido la hondura de tu desolación.

El dios de los hombres
no oye,
no ve,
no quiere saber nada de tu dolor.

Ese dios de corazón metálico y frío,
amado por los poderosos de la tierra,
es sordo a tu voluntad
y no quiere saber nada de Tu Reino.
Se inventa muchas razones
y una doctrina adecuada
para cada situación.

A Tí, en cambio,
te duele la condición indeseable
de las multitudes pobres,
que no tienen dinero,
pero que se sienten comidas en su vientre
por el dolor perenne
del hambre de cada día...

Te duele, Padre,
la extrema pobreza de las viudas
y de los huérfanos;
hechas viudas y huérfanos
por los generales de Guatemala.

FATHER, YOUR WOUNDED HEART

I know your wounded heart, Father.
I have heard you moan, like old Job,
I have listened to your sobs
and I have felt the depths of your desolation.

The god men worship
doesn't hear,
doesn't see,
doesn't want to know your pain.

The god with the cold, metallic heart,
loved by the powerful of the earth,
is deaf to your will
and wants to know nothing of your Kingdom.
The powerful rationalize
and devise a doctrine
suitable for every situation.

You, on the other hand, feel hurt
by the intolerable condition
of the poor multitudes
who have no money
and feel eaten up by the constant pain
of the hunger of every day ...

It hurts you, Father,
the extreme poverty of the widows
and the orphans,
widowed and orphaned
by the Generals of Guatemala,

de Chile,
de Paraguay,
de Haití
o de Namibia.

Te duele el corazón, Padre,
porque los cristianos
blancos, adinerados
y protestantes,
adoran en los Estados Unidos,
a un dios blanco,
metalizado y fundamentalista
en templos muy costosos
en donde no se aceptan negros...

Y en Africa del Sur,
tu clamas,
lloras,
peleas,
gritas, con tu dolor sin igual,
como Job,
mientras el dios europeo
de los blancos de occidente,
les sigue exigiendo inclemente,
para poder existir,
el sacrificio de muchos hermanos negros,
exterminados por hombres blancos,
adinerados y poderosos.

Yo siento adentro de mi pecho,
el dolor infinito de tu corazón oprimido, Padre,
porque muchos cristianos
en las cúpulas de las Iglesias,
temen mucho más a ese ídolo
que los sostiene satisfechos
en sus cargos de prestigio
que herir tu corazón
de Padre misericordioso y compasivo.

Te duele el corazón, Padre,
porque los que gobiernan

of Chile,
of Paraguay,
of Haiti,
of Namibia.

Your heart is hurting, Father,
because the Christians,
white, wealthy,
and Protestant,
worship in the United States
a white god,
metallic, fundamentalist,
in costly churches,
where blacks are not welcome.

And in South Africa,
you are shouting,
weeping,
fighting,
crying, in incomparable pain
like Job,
while the European god
of the Western whites
goes on harshly demanding,
for existence,
the sacrifice of many Black brothers and sisters,
exterminated by men,
white, wealthy and powerful.

I feel within my breast
the infinite pain of your oppressed heart, Father,
because many Christians
in the high offices of the churches
fear much more the idol
that keeps them happy
in their places of prestige
than they fear wounding the heart
of our merciful, compassionate Father.

Your heart is hurting, Father,
because those who govern

y dirigen a los pueblos
los someten y se sirven de ellos
amasando poder y prestigio
con sangre inocente.
Ellos prefieren a Mammón y a Baal
y te menosprecian a Tí, Padre,
Dador de la Vida.

Ellos te acusan
de ser un dios comunista,
porque odian *Tu Palabra*
y se han apropiado por la fuerza
de *Tu Tierra* y de todos sus recursos
como hicieron con la túnica de Jesús,
cambiando la vida del débil
por mucho menos que 30 monedas de plata.

Ellos quieren expulsar de *Tu Casa*
a los pobres,
a los que ahora lloran,
a todos los humildes
a los que padecen hambre y frío.
Y a todos aquellos
que trabajan por la justicia y la paz,
los calumnian, los persiguen y los matan
acusándolos de subversivos.

Ellos, como hijos legítimos del Malo,
no quieren escucharte,
no quieren saber que todo aquel
que se enseñorea de su hermano,
es como Caín, un homicida.

Por eso te duele el corazón, Padre,
y yo lo siento gemir en mi pecho,
y me repito en el silencio de la noche:

"Bienaventurados los misericordiosos,
porque ellos alcanzarán misericordia.
Bienaventurados si esos hombres os odian,

and lead the peoples
subdue them and take advantage of them
amassing power and prestige
with innocent blood.
They prefer Mammon and Baal,
despising you, Father,
Giver of Life.

They accuse you of being
a communist god,
because they hate Your Word
and have taken by force
Your Earth and all its resources
as they did with Jesus' tunic,
exchanging the life of the helpless
for much less than 30 silver coins.

They would chase the poor out of your house,
the ones who are crying,
the humble ones,
those who suffer hunger and cold.
And all those
who work for justice and peace
they slander, persecute, murder,
and accuse them of being subversives.

As the legitimate sons of evil,
they will not listen to you,
they don't want to know that anyone
who dominates his brother
is, like Cain, a murderer.

For this your heart aches, Father,
and I can feel it moaning in my breast,
and in the silence of night I repeat:

"Blessed are the merciful
for they shall attain mercy.
Blessed are you when men hate you

si proscriben o expulsan
vuestro nombre como infame...

Regocijaos y exultad,
porque entonces,
grande será vuestra recompensa,
así trataron sus padres a los profetas,
ésa es la señal
de que vosotros sois hijos
de vuestro Padre Misericordioso,"
el Dios de la Vida!

México
Marzo 31 de 1987

and persecute you and utter
every kind of slander against you ...

Be glad and rejoice,
for your reward
will be great;
thus your fathers treated the prophets,
and it is the sign
that you are the children
of your Merciful Father"
the God of Life!

Mexico
March 31, 1987

TEMBLOR

Tengo miedo, Señor.

Tengo miedo del miedo de los poderosos
de la inseguridad de los burócratas,
de la egolatría de los machos,
de aquellos que disponen,
con soberbia,
y en tu nombre,
de dinero y prestigio a su antojo.

Ellos, como Anás y Caifás
o como Herodes o Pilatos
siempre están disponibles
para prepararte de nuevo una cruz.

Ellos, los importantes,
anteponen su prestigio
a la desnuda y vergonzosa verdad.

Ellos, tienen miedo del riesgo, Señor.
Su posición les es demasiado preciosa.
Prefieren cavar bien una fosa
para hacernos desaparecer.

Ellos, Tú lo sabes bien,
hablan de justicia,
son muy honorables, y pulcros...
pero con sus hechos
traman la caída del justo
(y si es mujer, con mayor gusto).

A TREMBLING

I am afraid, Lord.

I am afraid of the fear of the powerful
        of the bureaucrats' insecurity,
        of the self-idolizing macho men,
        those who in their arrogance
        and in your name
        dispense money and influence
        at their whim.

Like Annas and Caiaphas,
like Herod or Pilate,
they are always there
to prepare your next cross.

The important ones,
they prefer their prestige
to the naked, shameful truth.

They are afraid to take a chance, Lord.
Their position is too precious.
They would rather dig a good, deep grave
to make us disappear.

You know very well
how they talk of justice,
they are very honorable, decent
but with their actions
they plot the fall of the just
(and if it is a woman, with greater pleasure).

Señor, líbrame
de caer en las redes
del hombre soberbio
y abre ante mis ojos
un camino de paz.

Caminaré contigo
por la senda antigua.
Cierra, te lo ruego,
fuertemente mi mano a la tuya
hasta que pueda hacer mía
aquella herida
abierta por el clavo
que te adhirió a la cruz.

Aquella herida tuya,
Infinita como tu amor,
herida posible,
porque uno de tus amigos
se dejó seducir por el proyecto sacerdotal
y sucumbió complaciente
ante el brillo fatuo
de la limosna institucional.

¡Necio amigo tuyo!
¿de qué le valió,
ya perdida su alma,
arrojar el ídolo
en un templo vacío de Dios?

¡Algo maravilloso ha ocurrido!
Ya no tengo miedo, Señor,
siento tu mano marcada,
ligada firmemente
a la mía pequeña.

Tu herida es la mía,
infinita...

En memoria del padre Rutilio Grande
Grandchamp
Marzo 19 de 1986

Lord, deliver me
from falling into the traps
of arrogant men
and open before my eyes
a path of peace.

I will walk with you
along the ancient path.
Grasp my hand firmly, I beg you,
in yours,
until your wound is mine,
opened up by the nail
that fixed you to the cross.

Your wound,
infinite as your love,
your wound happened
because one of your friends
fell for the scheme of the priests
and complacently gave in
before the fatuous gleam
of institutional charity.

Your foolish friend!
What good was it to him,
his soul already lost,
to cast out the idol
in a temple empty of God?

Something wonderful has happened!
I'm not afraid now, Lord,
I feel your scarred hand
firmly clasping
my little hand.

Your wound is mine,
infinite ...

In memory of Fr. Rutilio Grande
Grandchamp
March 19, 1986

POWER
OF
THE POOR

~

IN YOUR PATH
FOR THE CHRIST SCULPTED BY EDGAR
REVELATION
POWER OF THE POOR
LITTLE BROTHER
AND YOU, WHO DO YOU SAY IS THE
SON OF MAN?

EN TUS CAMINOS

Amo todos tus caminos
que me conducen a tu Casa, Señor,
caminos sencillos,
polvorientos,
descuidados,
y sembrados de viviendas sencillas.
Caminos subdesarrollados,
marcados por los pasos
de gente trabajadora:
constructores de anchas carreteras,
de casas ricas,
de jardines
y de parques.

Amo esos caminos
abandonados a la lluvia
y a la buena voluntad
de sus moradores disminuidos.
Caminos que me conducen
a la mujer analfabeta,
al niño sin escuela
y al viejo que vende helados
en su desgastada carretilla de madera.

Amo esos caminos
sin buena apariencia
ni atractivo,
que me conducen hasta tus hermanos
porque Tú, pobre con ellos,
me hablas desde su indigencia
y sacudes con violencia
todas mis seguridades
para aprisionarme inescapable

IN YOUR PATH

I love all your paths
that lead me to your House, Lord,
simple roads
dusty
neglected
bordered by simple houses.
Undeveloped roads
marked by the footprints
of working people:
builders of broad highways,
fancy houses,
gardens
and parks.

I love those paths
open to the rain
and to the good will
of their discounted residents.
Paths that lead me to the illiterate woman,
to the child who has no school,
to the old man who sells ice cream
from his worn-out wooden cart.

I love those paths
unimpressive
unattractive
that lead me to your brothers and sisters,
because You, poor with them,
speak to me from their indigence
and violently shake loose
all my assurances
binding me inescapably

en la secreta ternura
de tu desconocido sufrimiento.

Entonces me siento tu amiga,
porque me revelas todos tus secretos,
los secretos de un amor sin medida!

México
Septiembre de 1986

into the secret tenderness
of your unknown suffering.

And so I know I am your friend,
because you reveal your secrets to me,
the secrets of a love without measure!

Mexico City
September 1986

PARA EL CRISTO ESCULPIDO
POR EDGAR

Cristo - Pueblo,
Cristo - Indio,
Cristo - Fuerza de trabajo productiva,
Cristo - Sudor amargo en la costa sur,
Cristo - Raíz de tierra seca,
Cristo - Ayuno de Aqua Velva y de afeites,
Cristo - Dolor sin nombre
Cristo - Vergonzoso deshecho de los poderosos
Cristo - Milpa, mil veces destrozada
por la bota de los generales.

Te contemplo desde la Cruz
que te cargó el Capital,
y tu cuerpo-harapo
de jornalero
cortador de caña
o de algodón,
cansado,
sereno,
tranquilo,
sonriente,
y tu agonía de siglos,
lluvia abundante
de mis ojos,
fecunda mi tierra
de esperanza.

Contemplándote,
percibo por todas mis células
hasta el más recóndito

FOR THE CHRIST SCULPTED
BY EDGAR

Christ - the People
Christ - the Indian
Christ - the Strength of productive labor
Christ - the bitter Sweat of the southern coast
Christ - the Root of parched earth
Christ - the abstinence of Aqua Velva and
          cosmetics
Christ - nameless Sorrow
Christ - shameful undoing of the powerful
Christ - the Cornfield, a thousand times trampled
by the Generals' boots.

I gaze at you from the Cross
laid on you by Capital,
and your ragged body
day laborer
cane cutter
cotton picker,
tired,
serene,
tranquil,
smiling,
and your agony of centuries
rains from my eyes
abundantly
fertilizing my land
with hope.

Contemplating you,
I perceive with my every cell,
to the most hidden depths

rincón de mi conciencia
que,
inexorablemente,
y en contra de mil imperios,
los humildes como Tú,
heredarán la Tierra...

Y soy feliz!

Septiembre de 1984

of my consciousness,
that,
inexorably
and against a thousand empires,
the humble ones like You
will inherit the Earth ...

And I am happy!

September 1984

REVELACION

Las palabras del pobre
son cuchillos
que se hunden en nuestra carne
y cortan,
y duelen,
para dejar salir
la materia infecta.

El llanto del pobre
es agua clara
que lava cualquier maquillaje;
dejemos caer la máscara.

Los ojos del pobre
son dos espejos,
no tengamos miedo
de mirarnos en ellos.

La cercanía del pobre
nos revela a Jesús,
Consejero excelente,
Dios con nosotros,
Príncipe de Paz,
Fuego que quema
toda paja
y purifica el oro!

New Jersey
Julio 14 de 1984

REVELATION

The words of the poor
are knives
that bury themselves in our flesh
and cut,
and hurt,
and draw out
infection.

The cry of the poor
is clear water
that rinses off our makeup;
we can let the mask fall.

The eyes of the poor
are two mirrors,
we need not be afraid
to see ourselves there.

The nearness of the poor
reveals Jesus,
excellent Counselor,
God with us,
Prince of Peace,
Fire that burns away
all chaff
and purifies gold!

New Jersey
July 14, 1984

FUERZA DEL POBRE

ESE INEXPLICABLE,
ESE INDEFINIBLE...!
La irrupción de lo posible
en lo imposible.
Fuerza irresistible
que me empuja a gustar
el terrible vacío de la muerte.

Muerte convertida en Resurrección,
fuerza del débil para ascender
esa "montaña, que es algo más
que una inmensa estepa verde".[1]

Tradición rescatadora
de la Historia.
Protesta temeraria
contra la miseria
impuesta a fuego y sangre
por el rico insolente.

Asunción de la esclavitud
humana, que libera
y se hace liberación.
Obediencia absoluta al Amor
que se abraza enloquecida
a la muerte violenta de la Cruz.

Total abandono del Padre,
grito desgarrador...
sello imborrable de un amor
más fuerte que la muerte.
Torrente de vida inacabable,

POWER OF THE POOR

This inexplicable,
This undefinable...!
The bursting of the possible
through the impossible.
Unstoppable strength
that impels me to taste
the terrible emptiness of death.

Death changed into resurrection,
the power of the weak to climb
that "mountain which is something more
than an immense green steppe."[1]

Tradition that salvages
our History.
Bold protest
against misery
imposed by the insolent rich
with fire and blood.

Holy assumption of human slavery,
which liberates,
becoming liberation.
Absolute obedience to Love
which madly embraces
the violent death of the Cross.

Total abandonment of the Father,
rending cry ...
indelible seal of a love
stronger than death.
Uncontainable torrent of life,

generador de carne y sangre
que se hace nuestro hermano en el pobre.

Abrazo que mata y vivifica,
que quema sanando y
sacia la abrasadora sed de la existencia.
Presentimiento de la inmensidad
en la sencillez de lo pequeño.

Suiza
1987

---

[1] Título de un libro del comandante sandinista Omar Cabezas.

generating flesh and blood,
becoming the poor, our brother and sister.

Embrace that kills and gives life,
that heals by burning and
quenches the parching thirst of existence.
Presentiment of immensity
in the simplicity of the small.

Switzerland
1987

---

[1] Title of a book by the Sandinista commander Omar Cabezas.

HERMANO PEQUEÑITO

Para Pablito niño combatiente,
quien con su testimonio me enseñó muchas cosas
en febrero de 1982

Carita tímida y sonriente
de niño guerrillero,
vocecita de gorrión madrugador,
pupilas en perenne vigilia.

El glifo del hambre
ha escrito para siempre
el testimonio de la violencia
sobre tu piel anémica.

Tu historia sencilla
nos invita acogedora
a cerrar nuestras manos cansadas
con la tuya, ágil y certera,
por la vereda estrecha
que nos lleva hacia la libertad.

Los débiles chiribiscos
de tus brazos infantiles,
acogen cada día muerte,
para garantizarnos la vida.

Bajas a diario al abismo
de sombra y de muerte,
para traernos, desde allí,
el rayo de luz
que alimenta la esperanza.

LITTLE BROTHER

For Pablito, a child combatant
who with the testimony of his life
taught me many things during February 1982

Timid little smiling face
of the guerrilla child,
voice of the waking sparrow,
ever-vigilant pupils.

The mark of hunger
has written forever
proof of violence
on your anemic flesh.

Your simple story,
welcoming, invites us
to close our weary hands
around yours, agile and sure,
on the narrow trail
that leads us to freedom.

Your infant arms,
like sticks of kindling,
hug death every day,
to assure us of life.

Daily you brave the abyss
of shadow and death
to bring us, from the depths,
the ray of light
that feeds our hope.

Sé muy bien
que bajo tus harapos
"subversivos..."
guardas con cariño
la piedra y la honda
que derribará al gigante
un día no lejano.

Niño héroe,
de mi pueblo escarnecido
y condenado a la hoguera
en el nombre de Dios.

Niño pobre,
como el de Belén,
muchas veces lloro
de alegría y de dolor,
sintiendo desde lejos
tu carrera constante
evadiendo los *Pilatus*,
Los *Aravás* y los *Aerocommanders*
por barrancos y montañas.

Te veo muy bien desde aquí
abrazado a la tierra
con tu cuerpo delgado,
y cubrir con ella,
cuidadoso,
los cuerpos destrozados
de "nuestros hermanos pequeñitos"
de los que un día,
se sentarán a la diestra
del Padre de la Vida.

Niño indio,
débil tallo de violeta
que sostienes con tu aliento
nuestra débil fe
en el Sol de la Justicia.

I know
that under the rags
of a "subversive..."
you cradle the stone
and the slingshot
that will fell the giant
on a day not far away.

Child hero
of my scorned people
sentenced to burn
in the name of God.

Poor child
like the one in Bethlehem,
often I cry for joy
and sorrow,
sensing from afar
your constant flight,
evading the Pilatus,
the Aravas, and the Aerocommander planes
amid the ravines and mountains.

I can see you clearly from here,
your slight body
embracing the ground,
and with it covering,
carefully,
the devastated corpses
of our little brothers and sisters
who some day
will be seated at the right hand
of the Father of Life.

Indian child,
delicate sprig of violet
with your breath sustaining
our poor faith
in the sunshine of Justice.

En tu corazón agitado
por la lucha cotidiana
(por la existencia)
palpitan los milagros
de la alegría simple,
del perdón inexplicable
y de la lógica sencilla
que fluye del espíritu
de los genuinos Herederos del Reino,
que tanto aterran a Reagan
y a sus filisteos...

Tu trote acompasado
por valles y caminos,
golpea al mismo ritmo
mi corazón vigilante.
Y en esta larga noche
terriblemente oscura,
el Lucero del Alba
que resplandecía en tus ojos limpios
como de Epifanía,
me sigue iluminando!

El timbre de tu voz
aún no transformada,
es el clarín
que me despierta
cada mañana,
y me invita a continuar
la marcha pausada,
de los que no podemos
volar como tú,
pero podemos seguirte
desde el desierto,
caminando y caminando,
fortalecidos siempre
con el abastimento cotidiano
del maná
que brota gratuito
de tu corazón abierto

In your heart, stirred up
by the daily struggle
(for existence)
miracles throb
with pure joy,
with inexplicable forgiveness,
with the simple logic
that flows from the spirit
of the real Heirs of the Kingdom,
and frightens Reagan
and his Philistines ...

Your rhythmic pace
through the valleys and along the trails
beats in time with
my vigilant heart.
And through this long,
terribly dark night,
dawn's Morning Star
glows in your clear eyes
luminous
an Epiphany!

The timbre of your voice,
not yet changed,
is the reveille
that wakens me
every morning
and calls me to continue
our slow, deliberate march--
we cannot fly like you,
but we can follow
from the desert,
walking and walking,
strengthened always
by the daily provision
of manna
that bursts forth in abundance
from your open heart

sediento de JUSTICIA,
cuando nos confiesas
humilde y claramente
como el suave murmullo
de Yavé junto a la Cueva del Horeb:
que NO TE DEJARON CAMINO,
y que POR ESO,
TUVISTE QUE TOMAR
EL EXTRAVIO DE LA MUERTE,
que nos llevará algún día
a la "TIERRA PROMETIDA."

Diciembre 31 de 1982

thirsting for JUSTICE,
when you simply and clearly
confide to us
in the gentle whisper of Yahweh
before Horeb's Cave:
that THEY LEFT YOU WITHOUT A PATH,
AND SO,
YOU HAD TO CHOOSE
THE WILDERNESS OF DEATH,
which will lead us some day
to "THE PROMISED LAND."

December 31, 1982

Y TU, QUIEN DICES QUE ES EL HIJO DEL HOMBRE

Sí Señor,
yo sé bien quién eres
y en dónde estás.

Yo sé bien que naciste
en un pueblo ocupado militarmente
por el imperio de tu tiempo.

Sé también que una noche
saliste precipitadamente
huyendo de los soldados de Herodes
protegido en los brazos de tu madre,
porque aún no te había llegado la hora...

Eres el niño refugiado
en un país extranjero,
que sólo pudo volver
a la tierra añorada
cuando murió el colaborador del poder imperial.

Eres el amigo de los intocables,
marcados por la lepra,
El SIDA de tu época en Galilea.

Eres el Hijo de María,
la mujer fuerte del Magníficat,
Eres el carpintero de Nazareth
que rompiste las costumbres
convertidas en ley
por una cultura opresora.

Sí, eres el que te dejaste tocar
por la mujer pública,

AND YOU, WHO DO YOU SAY IS THE SON OF MAN?

Yes, my Lord,
I know very well who you are
and where you can be found.

I know very well that you were born
in a town militarily occupied
by the empire of your time.

I know too that one night
you left in a rush
fleeing Herod's soldiers
shielded in your mother's arms
because your hour had not yet come ...

You are the refugee child
in a foreign country
who could only return
to the land you longed for
when death struck down the agent of imperial
power.

You are a friend to the untouchables,
stigmatized by leprosy,
the AIDS of your epoch in Galilee.

You are the Son of Mary,
powerful woman of the Magnificat,
You are the carpenter from Nazareth
who shattered the customs
that the oppressive culture
had turned into laws.

Yes, you are the one who let the prostitute
touch you

porque percibiste,
más allá de toda racionalización,
el motivo último de su llanto
que alivió tus pies cansados
de exiliado en tu propia tierra.
Ella supo acoger tu corazón
de rechazado e incomprendido,
de profeta auténtico.

Yo sé quién eres,
el amigo de los pecadores,
porque nos escandalizas
al afirmar categórico,
que las prostitutas y los ladrones
van muy adelante de nosotros
en el camino sembrado de espinas
que nos conduce hasta el Reino de tu Padre.

Yo sé muy bien quién eres
y sé exactamente en donde encontrarte:
en una celda oscura y húmeda
de una cárcel en Taiwán,
y en la de África del Sur
y en la de Chile
y también en aquella de El Salvador.

Sé que ahora mismo
estás entre la población civil
en la selva del Ixcán
resistiendo la violencia militar
y huyendo de los aviones Pilatus Porter,
cuya fábrica en Sarnen,
defiende el derecho a la "libre empresa"
por encima del derecho a la vida
de los indios de Guatemala...

Yo conozco dónde moras,
en la casita siempre vigilada
de Winnie Mandela,
y en la de las Domitilas Chungaras,
allá en las minas de Bolivia,

because you saw,
beyond all reason,
the underlying impulse of her cry,
which soothed your tired feet,
you who were exiled in your own country.
She knew how to receive
your rejected, misunderstood heart,
the heart of a true prophet.

I know very well who you are,
friend of sinners,
because you scandalize us
when you say categorically
that the prostitutes and the thieves
walk well ahead of us
on the thorn-strewn path that leads
to your Father's kingdom.

I know very well who you are
and I know exactly where I'll find you:
in a dark, damp cell
in a Taiwanese prison
in a South African prison
in a Chilean prison
in a Salvadoran prison.

I know that even now
you are with the people
in the jungle of the Ixcan
resisting military violence
and fleeing the planes of Pilatus Porter
whose factory in Sarnen
defends the right of "free enterprise"
above the Guatemalan Indians'
right to life.

I know where you are staying,
in the always-watched house
of Winnie Mandela,
and in Domitilas Chungara's[1] house
in the Bolivian mines,

y en el barrio de los turcos:
"La Montaña de la Cruz",
en Berlín,
y entre los refugiados árabes,
en los territorios ocupados por Israel.
Yo te he visto entre los tamiles en Berna
y el domingo pasado,
te ví en una casita minúscula
de una costurera *min jung*
en un barrio mal oliente de Seúl.

Yo sé muy bien que sigues
viviendo donde mismo,
entre tus hermanos pequeñitos:
Los kanakos, los maorís
y los aborígenes pobres de Australia...
los que viven siempre con sed
y carecen de agua,
los que buscan algo rescatable
entre los basureros
y tienen que usar lo que otros deshechan.

Ya no insistas más, Señor,
te lo ruego,
yo sé hasta la saciedad,
que tú eres ciudadano del tercer mundo,
aquí en Corea del Sur o en París,
en la sierra ecuatoriana,
en el Harlem,
y en el *vía crucis* de Leonard Peltier
en los Estados Unidos.

Yo sé que perteneces a la raza ecuménica
de todos los disminuidos y oprimidos
del mundo entero.
Cuando me preguntas quién eres,
me pones entre la espada y la pared,
porque me preguntas en dónde estoy yo...

Pero yo también sé
que si te sigo paso a paso,

and in the Turkish neighborhood called
"The Hill of the Cross"
in Berlin,
and among the Arab refugees
in the Israeli-occupied territories.
I have seen you among the Tamils in Berne
and this past Sunday,
I saw you in a *min jung* seamstress'
tiny house
in a stinking slum in Seoul.

I know quite well that you
go on living wherever you are,
among your littlest brothers and sisters;
the Kanakos, the Maoris,
the poor Aborigines of Australia,
among those who live always thirsty,
needing water,
who look for something salvageable
in the garbage bins
and must use what others have thrown away.

Stop pressing me, Lord,
I beg you,
I know until I can't know any more
that you are a citizen of the third world,
here in South Korea or in Paris,
in the mountains of Ecuador,
in Harlem,
and in the *via crucis* of Leonard Peltier[2]
in the United States.

I know that you belong to the ecumenical race
of all the despised and oppressed
of the whole world.
When you ask me who you are,
you put me between a rock and a hard place,
because you ask me then where I can be found.

But I know, too,
that if I follow you step by step,

allí en donde moras
y a donde quiera que vayas,
me amenaza de muy cerca
el escándalo de la cruz
y la amargura de beber contigo del mismo cáliz...

Porque a tí,
te acusaron de alborotador
y de subversivo,
de blasfemo
y de actuar bajo el poder del demonio...

(¿que no harán conmigo, Señor?)

Dame tu coraje, te lo ruego,
ayúdame a recibir con el pan,
la cruz de cada día.

Concédeme la gracia
de seguirte de muy cerca,
cada instante de tu calvario y de tu muerte,
como Simón de Cirene
y aún más, como María,
con esa espada sembrada aquí, muy dentro...

Porque Señor,
quiero tener ojos muy limpios
para ser capaz de reconocerte de inmediato
la radiante mañana de Tu resurrección!

Seúl, Corea
Agosto 24 de 1989

there where you are staying,
and wherever you go,
I will be threatened at close range
by the scandal of the cross
and the bitterness of drinking with you from the
same cup ...

Because they accused you
of inciting riots,
of being a subversive,
of blasphemy
and even of carrying out the Devil's will

(what won't they do to me, my Lord?)

Give me your courage, I beg you,
help me to receive with my bread
my daily cross.

Give me grace
to follow you closely
in every moment of your Calvary and your death,
like Simon of Cyrene,
even more, like Mary,
with the sword buried here, very deep

Because, my Lord,
I want my eyes to be very clear
so that I will recognize you instantly
on the radiant morning of Your resurrection!

Seoul, Korea
August 24, 1989

---

[1] The life of Domitila Barrios Chungara, a Bolivian woman whose
husband worked in the mines, formed the basis of *Let Me Speak*, published
by Monthly Review.
[2] Leonard Peltier is a member of the American Indian Movement (AIM)
who was unjustly accused of murder in the 1970s. He remains
imprisoned.

Where are they?

IN
SOLIDARITY

~

YO ESTUVE EN LIDICE

Yo estuve en Lídice.

Caminé lentamente
contemplando las rosas.

Rosas rojas, amarillas,
blancas, rosadas,
y lilas.

Sólo rosas...

Me detuve y me bebí sedienta
todo el lugar en donde estuvieron las casas,
las tiendas, las escuelas y la Iglesia.
Recorrí con la mirada
toda la alfombra verde
que cubre el pasado
y sentí el aliento de la muerte
sobre mi piel helada...

Después,
entré el museo...
miré los papeles de identificación
de algunos de los asesinados,
fotografías,
pedazos de ropa envejecidos por el tiempo,
pedazos de anteojos
y de otras pertenencias.

Escuché el relato
y reviví el horror de los niños
apretujados unos contra otros

I WAS IN LIDICE

I was in Lidice.[1]

I walked slowly
contemplating the roses.

Red and yellow roses,
white and pink,
and lilac.

Only roses

I stopped and drank thirstily
of this whole place, the houses,
stores, schools, and the Church.
I surveyed all
the green carpet
that covers the past
and felt death wafting
across my chilled skin.

Later,
I went into the museum
I saw the ID papers,
photographs
bits of timeworn clothing
fragments of eyeglasses
other belongings
of those who were assassinated.

I listened to the story
and relived the horror of children
crowded together,

con sus caritas pálidas por el hambre,
y los ojos increíblemente abiertos...

Oí los pasos
de los nazis
conduciéndolos hacia la muerte...

Sí, yo estuve en Lídice.

Ahora, con el corazón hecho un harapo,
pienso que los super-nazis
del Pentágono,
han fabricado más de 200 lídices
en mi pequeña Guatemala
amparados en el mercado diplomático
de la falsa democracia occidental.

Sí, yo conozco Lídice.

Vancouver
Julio 2 de 1983

their faces pale with hunger,
their eyes incredibly wide ...

I heard the footsteps
of the Nazis
driving them to death ...

Yes, I was in Lidice.

And now, my heart in shreds,
I think of the Super-Nazis
in the Pentagon
who have created more than 200 Lidices
in my little Guatemala
sheltered by the diplomatic marketplace
of false Western democracy.

Yes, I am familiar with Lidice.

Vancouver
July 2, 1983

---

[1] Lidice was a village in Czechoslavakia which was destroyed by the Nazis
in 1942 in revenge for the assassination of a high Nazi official.

UNA MATITA DE ROMERO

Y llegado el cumplimiento del tiempo
quiso Dios revelarnos a su Hijo
en la carne de "los condenados de la tierra"
y empezamos a conocer
por qué no había dolor
semejante al Tuyo.

Y palpamos con nuestras manos
tu miseria en la de ellos
y compartimos tus lágrimas
en sus sollozos entrecortados
por lo insoportable de su dolor.

Y su clamor
trastornó nuestra vida tranquila
reviviendo la raíz de nuestra fe.
Y nos despertamos a la Vida Verdadera
que es crisis
y conflicto
y camino de esperanza.

Y tu Espíritu
zarandeó nuestra conciencia
y sanó nuestros ojos
obnubilados por una "gracia barata"
aseguradora del cielo
y satisfecha en la tierra.

Y el más tímido de tus pastores
oyó tu voz
en el balbuceo entrecortado por el sollozo

THE LITTLE ROMERO[1] PLANT

And in the fullness of time
God chose to reveal His Son to us
in flesh, as "the wretched of the earth"
and we began to know
why there is no sorrow
quite like Yours.

And we explored with our hands
your pain in their pain
and we shared your tears in their
sobbing, stifled
by their overwhelming grief.

And their cries
upset our tranquil existence
renewing the roots of our faith.
And we were awakened to True Life
which is crisis
and conflict
and expectant journey.

And your Spirit
shook our consciousness
and healed our eyes
which had been clouded by "cheap grace,"
certain of heaven
and content on earth.

And the most timid of your shepherds
heard your voice
in the murmur stifled by sobs

de las madres de los desaparecidos
y se atrevió *a vivir*
al hacerse pobre con ellas.

E hizo suya la pasión
que te llevó a la cruz.

Y encendido en el celo de tu Amor
increpó con el ímpetu de Amós
a los que teniendo ojos no quieren ver
a los que teniendo oídos no quieren escuchar
a esos, que todavía, a sabiendas...
siguen usurpando tu nombre.

Y el pueblo pobre
reconoció Tu voz en su palabra.
Tu voz inconfundible entre mil, Señor,
espada aguda, de doble filo,
que penetra lo más sutil del pensamiento.

Y el rico insensato,
y el poderoso
y el grande...Caín,
tuvo miedo.

Y el amor del Buen Pastor
derrumbó con Tu Palabra
el menosprecio de "los que no son"
para avergonzar a los que creen ser.

Y fuimos testigos de tu poder
cuando a través de su voz
nos ordenaste no matar.

Y de nuevo,
Herodes y Pilatos se amistaron.
Y cualquier D'Abuisson y la CIA
se abrazaron
e hicieron proyectos...

Y un 24 de marzo de 1980
mientras anunciaba

of the mothers of the disappeared
and he dared *to live*
to become poor with them.

And he took up the passion
that brought you to the cross.

And burning in the heat of your Love,
with the fierceness of Amos he rebuked
those who having eyes will not see
those who having ears will not hear
those who, still, even knowing,
go on usurping your name.

And the poor
recognized in his words Your voice.
Unmistakable your voice, my Lord, among
thousands,
a sharp double-edged sword
that penetrates the most subtle thinking.

And the foolish rich man
the powerful
the great ... Cain,
he was afraid.

And the Good Shepherd's love
destroyed with your Word
the contempt for "those who are nobody"
to the shame of those who believe they are
somebody.

And we witnessed your power
when with his voice
you ordered us not to kill.

And once again
Herod and Pilate became allies.
Another D'Aubuisson, another CIA
embraced and set up their projects ...

And on the 24th of March 1980
while he was announcing that

que el día vendrá
cuando habrá "una mesa común para todos,
con manteles largos
como en esta Eucaristía,
cada uno con su taburete.
Y que para todos
llegará la mesa
el mantel y el con qué".

Una ráfaga
disparada de las fauces
de un fusil
made in U.S.A.
cortó por un instante, (solamente!)
Tu Palabra, Señor.

...llegado el cumplimiento del tiempo
Tu Palabra germina y germina
y se hace cosecha infinita
en el campo del mundo.

Y la matita
de Romero
nacida en un rincón
de América Central
se hace pan y vino
de la Solidaridad Internacional.

Tu Palabra permanece
porque ningún poder
en las galaxias,
o en la tierra,
imperial o nacional,
podrá destruir jamás
ninguno de tus propósitos.

¡Resucitó!

En memoria de Nuestro Obispo y Mártir:
Oscar Arnulfo Romero
Marzo 22 de 1986

the day was coming
when there would be "one table
for all, with one long tablecloth
like we have here in the Eucharist,
and each with his own place.
And everyone will share in this table,
and this tablecloth, and this simple meal."

Gunfire
sprayed from the muzzle
of a rifle
made in U.S.A.
cut off for an instant (only!)
Your Word, my Lord.

And in the fullness of time
your Word conceives, and germinates,
and prepares an infinite harvest
in the countrysides of the world.

And the little rosemary plant, Romero,
born in a corner of Central America
takes International Solidarity
and makes bread and wine.

Your Word lives on
because there is no power
in all the galaxies
nor on the earth,
be it empires or nations,
that can ever erase
one line of your plans.

He is risen!

In memory of our bishop and martyr Mons. Romero.
March 22, 1986

---

[1] Romero is the name both for the former Archbishop of El Salvador and
for a rosemary plant.

VICTORIA DE LA ROCA

*Monja Belemita, secuestrada por el Ejército de
Guatemala y acusada de guerrillera porque había
trabajado en Nicaragua. Nunca más volvió a aparecer.*

Desde que entregaste
tus cinco panes
y tus dos pececillos
para la multitud hambrienta,
llamarada de amor
encendida junto
al pesebre de Belem
fue tu vida Victoria.

Todo lo que eras y lo que tenías
tu vida pequeña de mujer sencilla,
todo lo pusiste en sus manos,
blancos lirios de primavera
horadados por su pasión.

Fuiste de hielo
para la voz que desde tu miedo
te proponía claudicar.

Fuiste llama perenne
para la entrega incondicional.

Guerrillera, sí,
de Aquel Amor irresistible
que vino a incendiar el mundo
y hundió la espada
dividiendo familias
y también iglesias.

VICTORIA DE LA ROCA

Bethlemite nun, kidnapped by the Guatemalan army
and accused of being a guerrilla because she had
worked in Nicaragua. She was never seen again.

From the moment you gave up
your five loaves
and two little fishes
for the hungry multitude,
your life has been, Victoria,
on fire with love
burning alongside
the manger of Bethlehem.

All that you were and all that you had,
your small, simple woman's life,
you put it all in his hands,
the white lilies of spring
pierced by his passion.

You were ice
to the voice that spoke from your fear
telling you to back down.

You were an eternal flame
for unconditionally surrendering yourself.

Guerrilla, yes,
of that Irresistible Love
that came to set the world on fire
and wielded the sword
dividing families,
and splitting churches.

Con los pies bien plantados
sobre Aquella Roca,
marchaste obediente al martirio
prefiriendo el amor a la misma vida.

Signo magnífico el de tu nombre
que nos invita a seguir Sus pasos
y a heredar tu grito
que no pudo ahogar la tempestad.
Tiemblan los poderosos,
les castañean los dientes,
pues construyeron sus sueños
sobre el fango movedizo
de las mismas ambiciones de Caín.

Victoria de la Roca,
promesa eterna
que nos llega desde el Edén
y se extiende más allá,
mucho más allá
de la fiebre de Hitler
o de la paranoia de Reagan.

Tu victoria es la nuestra, Victoria
para siempre presente!

Stony Point, N.Y.
Abril 28 de 1987

With your feet planted
upon that Rock,
you walked obediently to martyrdom,
preferring love even to life.

The sign of your name is magnificent,
inviting us to follow His footsteps
and inherit your cry
which the tempest could not drown.
The powerful tremble,
their teeth chatter,
for they built their dreams
on the slippery silt
of Cain's own ambitions.

Victoria de la Roca,
eternal promise
that reaches to us from Eden
and extends beyond,
far, far beyond
the fever of Hitler
or Reagan's paranoia.

Your victory is ours, Victoria,
with us forever!

Stony Point, New York
April 28, 1987

PREGUNTA

Gotas de dolor
Otto René son tus poemas,[1]
gotas de profundo amor,
cápsulas concentradas de tristeza
que nos heredaste
con tus ojos muy fijos
en la estrella roja
clavada en el pecho herido del Quetzal.

Poeta triste,
alma eternamente enamorada de la vida.
Subiste al Calvario
porque amaste a Guatemala
hasta la muerte.

Tu prolongada noche,
noche nuestra,
oscura y dolorosa,
bañada con el llanto de tus hijas.

Noche embarazada
de alboradas,
pesadilla de siglos
largo camino con la patria a cuestas.

Dime si desde allí
donde tus ojos velan
esperando la madrugada,
se vislumbra ya la salida de Nuestro Sol...

Suiza
Mayo de 1985

---

[1] Otto René Castillo, poeta guatemalteco que después de un exilio,
volvió a Guatemala, se integró a la guerrilla y murió en combate.

QUESTION

Your poems, Otto Rene,[1]
are drops of pain,
drops of profound love,
concentrated capsules of sadness
which you bequeathed to us
with your eyes fixed steadily
on the red star
fixed to the Quetzal's wounded breast.

Sad poet,
soul ever in love with life.
You climbed up Calvary
because you loved Guatemala
unto death.

Your prolonged night,
our night,
dark and painful,
bathed in your daughters' crying.

Night that would give birth to the sunrise,
nightmare of centuries
long journey
with the weight of the country on your shoulders.

Tell me whether from over there
where your eyes watch
waiting for the dawn,
you can catch a glimpse yet of our rising Sun ...

May 1985

---

[1]Otto Rene Castillo was a Guatemalan poet who returned from exile to
join the guerrillas. He died in combat. *Footnote in original.*

SOLIDARIO

Tus amigos dormían
embotados en el pesado sopor
de la inconsciencia
cuando se fundía
en tí la vida.

Enteramente sólo
pronunciaste el sí incondicional.

El peso aplastante de la cruz,
te deshizo el corazón
que se te salió por los poros
fertilizando nuestra tierra
de esperanza!

Septiembre 27 de 1985

IN SOLIDARITY

Your friends were asleep, dull
with the heavy drowsiness
of the unaware
while life was forging itself
in you.

Completely alone
you pronounced the unconditional yes.

The crushing weight of the cross
splintered your heart,
which seeped through your pores
fertilizing our land
with hope!

September 27, 1985

EL BAUTISTA

"Voz que clama en el desierto"
Espada de dos filos hundida en mi carne y en la
        tuya
Hondo dolor, Juan, muy hondo!

Clamor amoroso del Dios de Israel
lámpara que arde en el camino hacia el Reino,
Amigo del esposo, gozo perfecto.

Celo exigente y radical de Yavé,
Visión del Amor de los amores
convertido en cordero
destinado al matadero.

Paloma posada sobre la Ofrenda Perfecta,
Fuego devorador de Dios
inflamando el corazón de mi pueblo
convertido en zarza que arde incesante.

¡Por mi causa y por la tuya...!

Diciembre de 1984

THE BAPTIST

"Voice crying in the desert"
Double-edged sword buried deep in my flesh and
       yours
Deep pain, John, very deep!

Loving cry of the God of Israel
lamp that blazes on the road to the Kingdom,
Friend of the groom, perfect joy.

Yahweh's jealousy, radical, demanding,
Vision of the Love among loves
converted into a lamb
destined for slaughter.

Dove poised above the Perfect Offering,
consuming Fire of God
setting afire the heart of my people,
becoming a bush that burns incessantly.

For my cause, and for yours!

December 1984

EUCARISTIA

Te vaciaste todo
sin retener nada para Tí.

Ya desnudo, total despojo,
te nos das hecho pan
que sostiene
y vino que reconforta.

Eres Luz y Verdad
Camino y Esperanza

Eres Amor

Crece en nosotros, Señor!

Octubre 5 de 1984

EUCHARIST

You emptied yourself completely
keeping nothing for Yourself.

Now naked, utterly stripped,
you give yourself to us as bread
which sustains us
and as wine that consoles us.

You are Light and Truth
You are the Way and the Hope

You are Love

Grow in us, Lord!

October 5, 1984

DIOS TE SALVE, MARIA

Duro tu camino, María,
estrecho y lleno de espinas.
Con el sí a tu elección,
recibiste también la cruz,
dolor convertido en júbilo
la límpida mañana
de nuestra resurrección.

Dios te salve
y en salvándote a tí,
nos salva en tu vientre fecundo.

Llena eres de gracia,
vaso de arcilla humilde
que siento palpitar en mi carne.

El Señor es contigo para siempre
desposorio santo,
Alianza eterna
que nos rescata cada día
de la senda extraviada
de nuestro adulterio.

Bendita tú eres
entre todas las mujeres
porque todas recibimos de tí
la plenitud de la gracia.

Bendito el fruto del Amor
que ilumina nuestras oscuridades
y nos conduce hacia la Aurora Perfecta.

México
Julio de 1985

AVE MARIA

Your path is hard, Mary,
narrow and full of thorns.
Answering "yes" to the call,
you also received the cross,
sorrow into joy,
the pure, clear morning
of our resurrection.

Hail! God save you, Mary,
and in saving you, save us
in your fruitful womb.

Full of grace are you,
vessel of humble clay
throbbing in my own flesh.

The Lord is with you for all time
holy betrothal,
eternal Alliance
that rescues us daily
from the wayward path
of our adultery.

Blessed are you
among women
because all women receive in you
the fullness of grace.

Blessed is the fruit of Love
that illumines our darkness
and leads us to the perfect Dawn.

Mexico
July 1985

LA IGLESIA

Esa virgen pura
en espera del esposo,
vigilante y presurosa
Fuente sellada
y corazón vigilante.
Bella como la luna.

Esa prostituta
entregada a sus amantes
Esa, de cuya boca
El que está locamente enamorado de ella
sacará para siempre
el nombre de Baal.

Esa virgen, esa prostituta
muy adentro de nosotros
en opción por Jesús o contra El
en nuestra relación con los pobres.

THE CHURCH

Pure virgin
waiting for her spouse,
vigilant and anxious
sealed fountain
and vigilant heart.
Beautiful as the moon.

Prostitute
surrendered to her lovers
She, from whose mouth
the One who is madly in love with her
will perpetually remove
the name of Baal.

Virgin, prostitute
very deep within us
making the option with Jesus, or against Him
in our relations with the poor.

¡QUE PENA ME DA!

Cuando la luz
apenas empieza a disipar la noche,
despierto con el Gloria
cantando a todo pulmón
por todos los gallos de Managua.

Las gotas de lluvia
caen de tanto en tanto
de las hojas del limonar...

Viene claramente a mi conciencia
aquella otra madrugada,
en el patio de la casa del Sumo Sacerdote
y oigo los sollozos de Pedro
antes de que lo nombraran Papa.

Qué pena me da la existencia
de tantos obispos, cardenales,
pastores, curas,
y etc., etc.,
con el alma más parecida
a la de Anás y Caifás
que a la de Pedro,
antes de que lo nombraran Papa.

¡Qué pena me da!

Nueva Nicaragua
Octubre 13 de 1988

HOW ASHAMED I AM!

When the light
has barely begun to dissipate the night,
I wake up to the Gloria
sung by all the roosters of Managua
at the top of their lungs.

Rain falls
drop by drop
from the leaves of the lemon tree

Into my mind comes clearly
that other daybreak
in the patio of the High Priest's house
and I can hear the sobs of Peter
before they named him Pope.

How it shames me, the existence
of so many bishops, cardinals,
pastors, priests,
etc., etc.,
with souls more similar
to those of Annas and Caiaphas
than to that of Peter
before they named him Pope.

How ashamed I am!

Nicaragua
October 13, 1988

SEMEJANZA

Si de verdad
los cristianos
creyéramos que somos un solo Cuerpo,
el de Cristo Resucitado,
¡Cuántas situaciones podríamos cambiar!

Esa pequeña semilla de mostaza
reventaría la roca más dura
y trasladaríamos las montañas de la riqueza
para rellenar los barrancos de la miseria.

¡Púchica, si hasta viviríamos
como hermanos verdaderos!
Y la tierra con todos sus tesoros
sería el Pan Nuestro de cada día
y nunca más tomaríamos el nombre
de Nuestro Padre en vano.

A veces,
la posibilidad de hacer HISTORIA
el mayor de los mandamientos,
se asemeja mucho a ciertas utopías.

¿Será por eso que se persigue y se mata
a los que de verdad creen
e intentan vivir su fe?

Vancouver
Julio de 1983

RESEMBLANCE

If Christians
really believed
that we are one single Body,
that of the Risen Christ,
how many situations we could change!

That little mustard seed
could split the hardest rock,
and we could move mountains of wealth
to fill in ravines of misery.

Goodness! If we even lived
like true brothers and sisters!
And the land with all its treasures
would be our Daily Bread
and never again would we take
Our Father's name in vain.

At times,
the possibility of making HISTORY
the greatest of the commandments
closely resembles utopia.

Would that be why they persecute and kill
those who really believe
and try to live their faith?

Vancouver
July 1983

¡EN MARCHA!

Tarea titánica,
divina tarea, la nuestra:
hacernos humanos!

¡En marcha!
derribando ídolos
rompiendo cadenas,
desapegándonos!

¡En marcha!
despojo constante,
avanzar, tropezar, caer,
levantarse!
Avanzar!

Fija la mirada siempre en la utopía,
en aquel paraíso perdido
presente siempre y siempre distante.
Imán poderoso,
fuerza desconocida, negada, atacada
por los anti-hombres.

Vocación, primera,
postrera,
mil veces perdida
y otras mil encontrada.

Unica posibilidad
de ser con sentido
para conocer la Vida
y conjugarla en lo más íntimo,
iluminados!

Managua
Noviembre 4 de 1988

ON THE MARCH!

Titanic task,
a divine task, ours:
to make ourselves human!

On the march!
knocking down idols
breaking chains
tearing free!

On the march!
Relinquishing ourselves,
advancing, stumbling, falling,
and rising again!
Moving on!

Fix your eyes always on utopia,
on that lost paradise
always present and always distant.
Powerful magnet,
unrecognized strength, denied, attacked
by the anti-humans.

Vocation, first
and final,
a thousand times lost
a thousand times found.

Sole possibility
to live with meaning,
to know Life
to fuse with her intimately,
illuminated!

Managua
November 4, 1988

ANHELO

Quiera yo querer lo que tú quieres,
amar lo que amas
y aborrecer lo que aborreces.

Quiera yo vivir tu vida
y morir tu muerte,
fundirme toda en ti
y ser en ti una sola voluntad,
un solo corazón
para hacer camino sobre tus huellas
de Peregrino Eterno.

Quieras Tú concederme
el supremo don
de amarte con tu amor
y la bendita gracia
de sufrir tu sufrimiento,
combatir tu combate
y cantar tus alabanzas
todos los días de mi vida.

¿Qué otra gloria podrá consolar
mi alma sedienta
de todo lo que Tú sólo eres?

Grandchamp, Suiza
Agosto 18 de 1986

LONGING

Would that I want what you want,
love what you love,
and hate whatever you hate.

Would that I would like to live your life
and die your death,
become one with you
and be with you one single will,
one heart
so as to follow in your footsteps,
Eternal Pilgrim.

And would that you give me
the supreme gift
of loving you with your love
and the blessed grace
of suffering with your suffering
fighting your fight
singing your praises
all the days of my life.

What other glory could soothe
a soul that is thirsty
for all that only You are?

Grandchamp, Switzerland
August 18, 1986

VEN AMOR

De la palabra callada,
de la lágrima jamás vertida,
del suspiro ahogado,
del anhelo escondido,
de lo más hondo del dolor,
desde allí Amor,
clavada al pie de tu Cruz,
yo cuento los instantes
prolongados al infinito
hasta tu venida!

Con el fango hasta el cuello
y los ojos puestos en Tu Reino,
Con la nostalgia de ser quemada por tu luz
y el alma plena de futuro,
Yo te grito, Ven, ven Amor,
que tu abrazo tan temido
me consuma
y que fundida en Tí
pueda anunciar al mundo
¡Maranatha, El ya está aquí!

Octubre 5 de 1984

COME, LOVE

From the silenced word,
the unwept tear,
the sigh choked back,
the hidden desire,
from the deepest pain,
from there, Love,
nailed to the foot of your Cross,
I count the infinitely
stretching instants
until your Coming!

Up to my neck in slime
I keep my eyes fixed on Your Kingdom,
Longing to be burned by your light,
my soul filled with the future
I cry out to you, Come, come, my Love,
may your much-feared embrace
consume me
and, fused with You,
may I then be able to announce to the world,
Maranatha! He is already here!

October 5, 1984

MANOJITO DE MIRRA

Me habitas, Amor,
como manojito de mirra
entre mis pechos.
Exigente, dolorosa, agónico,
como tu "Sí" al Padre
la noche oscura de Getsemaní,
manso, humilde,
como cordero destinado al sacrificio.

El aliento de tu boca
asciende constante desde mi pecho
impregnándome toda
del aroma de tu pasión.

Mirra adorada,
Cordero,
necesito de tu hálito cada instante
para discernir el Camino de tu Cruz
y para reconocerte siempre
de pie, junto al sepulcro,
!lirio inmaculado de los valles,
todo vestido de luz!

Flueli-Ranft, Suiza
Agosto 9 de 1986

LITTLE BUNDLE OF MYRRH

You live in me, my Love,
like a little bundle of myrrh
between my breasts.
Demanding, sorrowful, agonized,
like your "yes" to the Father
Gethsemane's dark night,
humble, gentle,
like a lamb destined for sacrifice.

The breath from your mouth
ascends constantly from my breast
impregnating me completely
with the aroma of your passion.

Precious myrrh,
my lamb,
I need your breath every moment
to discern the Way of your Cross
and to recognize you always
standing, next to the tomb,
immaculate lily of the valley,
dressed all in light!

Flueli-Ranft, Switzerland
August 9, 1986

YUGO DULCE

Desde acá,
corro con los que corren,
con los que tiemblan y cantan,
con los que ríen y lloran,
con los que saturados de amor
comparten alegrías y tristezas,
raíces y tortillas,
enfermedad y fortaleza
sobre las montañas,
en las cuevas y barrancos
y en la loma pelada por el fuego
de la "tierra arrasada",
inventada para Viet Nam
y perfeccionada en Guatemala.

Desde el terrible verano de Washington,
siento el frío de la noche
que cubre solidaria
las marchas forzadas
de los sobrevivientes
huyendo hacia Chiapas.

Cuando golosa
olfateo los huipiles
de Todos Santos
o de San Ildefonso Ixtahuacán,
siento la mano cariñosa
que muele el nixtamal
acariciándome la cara
y ofreciéndome la tortilla
con un poco de sal.

SWEET YOKE

At a distance,
I run with those who are running,
with those who tremble and sing
with those who laugh and cry,
filled with love, sharing
joy and sadness,
tortillas and roots,
sickness and strength
across the mountains,
in caves and ravines,
on the hillsides stripped
by the fires of "scorched earth,"
invented for Viet Nam
and perfected in Guatemala.

From the terrible Washington summer,
I feel the night chill
giving cover
to forced marches
of survivors
fleeing toward Chiapas.

When I greedily
sniff the huipiles
of Todos Santos
or San Ildefonso Ixtahuacan,
I feel the loving hand
that grinds the nixtamal
stroking my face
and offering me a tortilla
with a little salt.

La sensación del humo, entonces,
me saca con las lágrimas,
el gemido de Carmen
que perdió su hijito
crucificado por el hambre
en un campamento de refugiados.

Oigo el chisporroteo del fuego
devorando los techos
y las frágiles paredes
de los ranchos ancestrales.
!Me abraza el corazón
el infierno que quema
la carne de los indios
quichés, kakchikeles, tztuhiles,
mames, kekchíes y pocomchíes!
Y siento las botas de la soldadesca
sobre mi pecho
pisando la milpa sagrada,
amorosamente cultivada
por los sembradores de la vida.

Sollozo silenciosa
con los patrulleros de Chiul
que cumplieron las órdenes de hermano Efraín
el 23 de marzo de 1982 en Parraxtut.

Y con mis manos temblorosas
muy adentro de la patria,
limpio la sangre coagulada
del cuello de los ancianos
degollados a golpes de hacha
para borrar su nombre de la historia,
y constato de nuevo,
sangre baja en hemoglobina,
casi agua,
como la que salió del costado de Jesús.

Then the sting of smoke
draws my tears, and with them
Carmen's wailing,
when she lost her little boy
crucified by hunger
in a refugee camp.

I hear the fire crackling,
devouring the roofs
and fragile walls
of ancestral huts.
It encircles my heart,
the fire that burns
Indian flesh
Quiches, Kakchikeles, Tztuhiles,
Mames, Kekchies and Pocomchies!
I feel the boots of the troops
crossing my breast,
flattening the sacred cornfield
lovingly nurtured
by the sowers of life.

I sob in silence
with the patrolmen of Chiul
who carried out Brother Efraín's orders
on March 23, 1982 in Parraxtut.[1]

And with trembling hands,
I reach deep inside my country
and wipe encrusted blood from the throats
of old men and women,
their heads cut off with ax-blows
so as to blot their names from history,
and I witness again
blood deficient in hemoglobin,
almost water,
like that which seeped from the side of Jesus.

Peregrina con mi pueblo,
camino su camino,
y sostenida por su aliento inextinguible,
subo la difícil cuesta del exilio
con los ojos puestos en la misma estrella
que ilumina el cielo extraordinariamente azul
sobre los picos de los volcanes,
desafiando el silencio
de esta noche oscura
para recordarnos
la Palabra Eterna
del Gran Zahorín,
"nuestra estirpe
no se extinguirá
mientras haya luz
en el Lucero de la Mañana."[1]

Washington/Vancouver
Junio/julio de 1983

---

[1] Palabras de Hunahpú-Ixbalanqué en el Pop Vuh, libro sagrado de
los Maya-Quichés.

Pilgrim with my people,
I walk their road,
and sustained by their inextinguishable breath,
I climb the steep path of exile
my eyes fixed on that star
which brightens the extraordinarily blue sky
above the peaks of volcanoes,
defying the silence
of this dark night,
reminding us of
the Eternal Words
of the Great *Zahorin*,[2]
"our lineage
will not be extinguished
as long as there is light
from the Morning Star."[3]

Vancouver/Washington
June/July 1983

---

[1] 500 villagers of Parraxtut were killed by the military-controlled civilian patrol of the neighboring village of Chiul on the day of the Ríos Montt coup (March 23, 1982).

[2] A *zahorin* is a traditional Mayan priest.

[3] Words of the Hunahpú in the Popul Vuh, holy book of the Maya-Quichés.

SISTER, WOMAN
OF
FAITH

~

RESURRECCION

Amo la vida,
el sol, el aullido del viento en la montaña
la tempestad, los truenos,
el canto alegre de los pájaros,
la alegría de los conejos,
el ladrido de los perros,
y el paseo de los caracoles
después de la lluvia.

Amo la vida,
el cante hondo del gitano rebelde,
el lamento ancestral de la flauta,
la danza violenta de los rusos
y la sonrisa tímida de los niños indios.

Amo la vida,
piel morena o blanca,
el brillo de las mejillas de los negros,
los cabellos que tienen el color
del pelo del maíz.
Amo las hormigas nunca ociosas,
el mugido de las vacas
y el tintineo de sus campanas
en el Alpes.

Amo la vida,
el zumbido de las abejas golosas,
las travesuras de las ardillas,
la piel maravillosa del zorro
la bella estampa del cervatillo
y la gallardía del caballo
con su melena al viento.

RESURRECTION

I am in love with life,
the sun, the howling of mountain winds,
the storm, the clap of thunder,
the songbirds' joyful singing,
the rabbits' delight,
the barking dogs,
and the promenade of the snails
after the rain.

I am in love with life,
the deep chant of rebel gypsies,
ancestral lament of the flute,
the violent dance of the Russians,
shy smile of the Indian children.

I am in love with life,
dark skin or white,
the shine of Black cheeks,
hair the color
of cornsilk.
I love the ants that never rest,
the lowing cows
and the sound of their bells
clanging in the Alps.

I am in love with life,
the buzzing of gluttonous bees
the mischievous squirrels
the fox's wonderful fur
the musk deer's beautiful form
and the gallantry of the horse
with his mane to the wind.

Amo la vida,
las violetas sencillas
que brotan como milagro
desafiando aún el hielo del invierno,
las pequeñas primaveras amarillas,
las anémonas delicadas y frescas,
los narcisos luminosos
y el aroma maravilloso
de las lilas penetrando por mi ventana.

Grandchamp, Suiza
Primavera de 1986

I am in love with life,
the plain little violets
appearing like a miracle
defying even the winter's ice,
the tiny yellow primroses,
delicate, fresh anemones,
luminous narcissus
and the wonderful aroma
of lilies pouring in through my window.

Grandchamp, Switzerland
Spring 1986

ALFARERO

El hombre,
pobre barro,
tosco y resistente,
no ha tomado todavía
entre tus manos,
forma humana.

Tú, incansable alfarero,
te empeñas paciente,
en volver a empezar
una y otra vez,
poco a poco,
lentamente,
eras,
siglos,
milenios.

Desde
Adán hasta Noé,
de Noé hasta Abraham
de Abraham hasta Moisés,
de Moisés hasta Jesús...

Y aún ahora,
quienes llevamos tu nombre
nos resistimos rudamente
retrasando tu obra,
la más amada,
por la que sufres
y te entregas.

THE POTTER

Man,
poor clay,
crude, resistant
still has not taken
human form
in your hands.

You, tireless potter,
patiently persist,
starting over
and over again
little by little,
slowly
eras
centuries
millennia.

Beginning
with Adam, then Noah,
from Noah to Abraham
from Abraham to Moses
from Moses to Jesus ...

And even now,
we who bear your name
stubbornly resist,
retarding your work,
your beloved creation,
the one for which you suffer
and sacrifice.

Cómo nos cuesta
ser modelados
entre tus manos
a tu imagen y semejanza!

Dios de la vida
y la Vida misma,
Señor de la Historia,
aquí estamos,
medio lobos y medio humanos,
aquí nos tienes,
no nos abandones
te rogamos,
vuélvenos a empezar!

Mayo 1 de 1986

How hard it is for us
to be shaped
in your hands,
in your image and likeness!

God of our lives
and of Life itself,
Lord of all History,
here we stand,
half wolf, half human,
here you have us,
do not leave us, we pray,
begin on us again!

May 1, 1986

YO NO SOY UNA POSEIDA

Para las muchas mujeres valientes
de mi Guatemala (San Juan 8:49)

Yo no soy una posesa,
yo no soy una loca
poseída por una idea fija.

Yo soy sólo una mujer
con un corazón humano.

Yo soy una rebelde
frente a la fría y calculada
corrección del funcionario...

Ese ser enmarcado siempre
entre los límites de "lo correcto"
"lo objetivo" y "lo prudente"
de un balance siempre neutral.

Ese que evita correr riesgos
en aras de su cargo
y de sus prestigio.

Yo soy poseedora
(no posesa)
de esa normalidad de mujer
que rechaza y rechazará siempre
el desorden constituido
por los machos
todos ellos generales en potencia.

I AM NOT POSSESSED!

For the many valiant women
of my Guatemala   (John 8:49)

I am not possessed
I am not crazy
obsessed with an idea.

I am simply a woman
with a human heart.

I am a rebel
when faced with the cold and calculated
correctness of a bureaucrat.

He who is always bound
by the limits of "the correct"
"the objective" and "the prudent"
of an always-neutral balance.

The one who avoids taking risks
for the sake of his office
and his prestige.

I am the possessor of
(not possessed by)
the normality of a woman
that rejects and always will reject
the disorder constituted
by *machos,*
all of them potential generals.

Por todos esos
que ponen la ley
por encima de la vida;
la institución
por encima de la humanidad,
el proyecto personal
por encima de la verdad,
el miedo
por encima del amor,
la ambición
por encima de la humildad.

Pero tengo que admitirlo,
para los obsesionados
por esos criterios,
yo soy una brasa
encendida por el fuego
de un gran amor.

Hermano,

¿Conoces el relato
de la zarza ardiente
que no se consumía?

Suiza
Marzo 20 de 1986

By all those
who place the law
above life;
the institution
above humanity,
the personal project
above truth,
fear
above love,
ambition
above humility.

But I must admit
to those obsessed
with such criteria,
I am a red-hot coal
lighted by the fire
of a great love.

Brother,

Do you know the story
of the burning bush
that was never consumed?

Switzerland
March 20, 1986

DECISION

Si
cuando desvelas al engaño
te hieren;
!agoniza,
no morirás!

Si
cuando dices la verdad
te matan;
!muere!
!Resucitarás!

Si
cuando caes,
te pisan y te aplastan;
!levántate,
caminarás!

Si
todo ha terminado
y te falta el aliento,
!Vuelve a empezar!

Agosto de 1984

RESOLUTION

If
when you shed light on the lies
they hurt you--
then feel the pain!
You will not die!

If
when you speak the truth
they kill you--
die, then!
You will rise again!

If
when you fall
they trample you and crush you--
stand up then!
You shall walk!

If
all is over and
you cannot even draw another breath,
Return, and begin again!

August 1984

ESPERA

Me duele la vida
por todos los que han muerto.

Me duele la alegría
por todos los que lloran.

Me duele el amor
por todos los que odian.

Y mientras amo, río y lloro
Yo te espero Señor.

WAITING

Life is painful
because of the ones who have died.

Joy is painful
because of the ones who are crying.

Love is painful
because of the ones who hate.

And while I am loving, laughing and crying,
I am waiting for you, my Lord!

COMPAÑERO

La Revolución, compañero,
no es tu brillante discurso
sin el sostén del estricto cumplimiento
de la sencilla tarea cotidiana.

La Revolución, no es tu brillante análisis
si le niegas el respaldo al compañero
que se esfuerza por servirle fiel al pueblo
que lucha y se desangra adentro.

La Revolución, no es carrera vertiginosa
sutil y hábil por llegar a tu propia meta
antes que los otros sin tenderle la mano
al amigo, a la mujer abandonada
y a todos los otros
que marchan infatigables hacia una sola meta.

La Revolución, no son palabras vacías
del contenido de toda una vida puesta al servicio
del hermano que intenta ponerse en marcha.
La Revolución no es cálculo solapado para salir
            siempre adelante,
sino crítica conjunta para parir un pueblo sano.

La Revolución, compañero, es enderezar tu vida
hacia el horizonte de LA VIDA profundamente
            humana,
al servicio del que sufre y lucha
y también del prójimo cercano que intenta
ponerse de pie para acompañar la lucha.

COMPAÑERO

The Revolution, *compañero*,
is not your brilliant discourse
without the disciplined performance
of simple daily tasks.

The Revolution is not your brilliant analysis
if you turn your back on a companion
who strives faithfully to serve the people,
while struggling and bleeding inside.

The Revolution is not a heady career
suitable for arriving at your own goals
ahead of the rest, without offering your hand
to a friend, to an abandoned woman,
to all the others
who walk without tiring towards one shared goal.

The Revolution is not meaningless words
about a life of service
to the brother who wants to join the march.
The Revolution is not a cunning calculation designed
            to get you ahead,
but rather collective criticism giving birth to a
            healthy people.

The Revolution, my friend, means directing your life
toward the horizon of the profoundly human LIFE
at the service of those who suffer and struggle
and of your closest neighbor who is trying
to stand up and join the struggle.

La Revolución, compañero,
es limpiarnos de nuestra propia mugre
para poder limpiar también la de los otros,
es crecer en conjunto
y así, aproximarnos a un futuro un poco más
humano.

París/New York
Mayo 1983

The Revolution, my friend,
means wiping our own filth away
so that we can clean others, too;
it means growing, together,
and thus drawing nearer to a somewhat more
humane future.

Paris/New York
May 1983

FRONTERA

Migración - límite
No estacionar - Frontera
Migración - límite
No estacionar - Frontera.
ALTO.
"Bienvenidos a Honduras
Tierra de Paz y Libertad"
ALTO
PRECAUCION
viento, viento, más viento
pequeñas gotas de lluvia,
lluvia fina,
constante que moja
que empapa, que cala...

Hacia el norte, nubes negras.

El clarín del gallo.
Sasamori,[1]
ritmo acompasado
persistente letanía,
palpitar profundo
al compás del corazón,
latiendo vida,
llanto,
amor,
oración,
venido de Oriente
como los Magos de Belem.

En mi alma: deseo profundo
de acercarme a jugar

BORDER

Immigration--Restricted Area
No Parking--Border
Immigration--Restricted Area
No Parking--Border
STOP.
"Welcome to Honduras
Land of Peace and Freedom"
STOP
CAUTION
steady wind blowing, harder,
tiny raindrops falling,
a fine rain,
incessant, soaking,
drenching, permeating ...

And to the north, black clouds.

The trumpet call of a rooster.
Sasamori[1]
measured beat
steady litany,
deep throbbing
to the beat of a heart,
pulsing life,
lamentation,
love,
prayer,
come from the East
like the Magi of Bethlehem.

In my soul: a profound yearning
to draw near and to play

con ese niño ensimismado y solo
de ojos bajos y tristes...
quebrar la frontera,
des-oír el alto
que lo aísla huraño
temeroso del regaño hostil,
ganarme su sonrisa
y palpitar amor.

pan pan-pan pan-pan pan pan
tambor persistente cercano distante

Na-Mu-Myo-Ho-Ren-Ge-Kyo
pan pan-pan pan-pan pan pan
pan pan-pan pan-pan pan pan

latido, gemido, cercano, distante
recuerdo - insistente
perenne - latente
constante - presente
chirimía - letanía
gemido - incesante
latido de siglos
retumbando en mi mente
tamborón, pon, pon
chirimía - gemido
retumbando siempre
en mi corazón pon pon
anhelante siempre!

Las Manos, Nicaragua
Diciembre 1-5 de 1988

---

[1] Monje budista japonés que marcha, ora, ayuna y reconstruye lo
destruído en Nicaragua, hasta que venga la paz.

with this solitary, introspective child, he
of the sad, downcast eyes ...
to break down the border,
to disregard the stop-sign
that keeps him shy and isolated,
fearful of hostile scolding,
to win for myself his smile,
to touch love.

boom-boom, boom-boom, boom-boom-boom
steady beating nearer further

Na-Mu-Myo-Ho-Ren-Ge-Kyo
boom-boom, boom-boom, boom-boom-boom
boom-boom, boom-boom, boom-boom-boom

pulsing, groaning, nearer, further,
memory - insistent
perennial - latent
continual - present
chirimia[2] - litany
groaning - incessant
the pulsing of centuries
echoes in my head
boom-boom, beating drum
wailing flute
echoing forever
in my heart, boom-boom
forever yearning!

Las Manos, Nicaragua

---

[1] Sasamori is a Japanese Buddhist monk who marched, prayed and fasted
for the reconstruction of Nicaragua following the destruction brought
about by the civil war. *Footnote in the original.*

[2] A type of flute.

HERMANA, MUJER DE FE

Aquí sentada
frente al Hudson
que separa a New Jersey
de la isla de Manhattan,
robada a los indios por 24 dólares,
medito en Babel...
y en sus machos altaneros
que intentaron alcanzar el cielo,
en su confusión y en su fracaso...

Mientras tanto,
Reagan nos amenaza
con un enemigo imaginario
y ofrece los misiles espaciales
que asegurarán la hegemonía
del Sheriff del Oeste
sobre el mundo.

Pienso en los indios
sacados a sangre y fuego de Manhattan,
y mi corazón estrujado
por el dolor,
intenta detener con otros
corazones solidarios,
las garras del capital
sobre Santiago Atitlán,
Panajachel,
Izabal,
el valle del Polochic,
Sayaxché,
Parraxtut,
Petanac,

SISTER, WOMAN OF FAITH

Seated here
beside the Hudson
that separates New Jersey
from the island of Manhattan,
stolen from the Indians for 24 dollars,
I think of Babel ...
and in their *macho* arrogance
they thought they could touch the sky,
in their confusion and in their ruin ...

Meanwhile,
Reagan threatens us
with an imaginary enemy
and offers space missiles
to ensure the hegemony
of the Sheriff of the West
over the world.

I think of the Indians
driven from Manhattan with blood and fire,
and my heart
crushed by sorrow
along with other hearts in solidarity
struggles to turn back
the claws of Capital
poised over Santiago Atitlan,[1]
Panajachel,
Izabal,
the Polochic valley,
Sayaxche,
Parraxtut,
Petanac,

el valle del Cauca...
Más adelante,
José Martí
me sale al paso:

"La Patria es ara, no pedestal."

Patria...
-- no la de los generales --
es la sangre de los indios
cuyo clamor me sacude las entrañas
desde los cimientos del *Empire State Building,*
Patria son los antepasados
de la población negra
cazados vivos
por los abuelos de Jorge Washington
y de Abraham Lincoln.

Patria son los negros
encadenados unos a otros como fieras
en los barcos holandeses
atravesando el océano
sin saber a dónde iban
y que, como Jesús,
murieron de sed
encadenados al mástil
de la Cruz.

Patria son los 30,000 indios
que en El Salvador
murieron masacrados en 1932
bajo el OK de la Casa Blanca.

the valley of the Cauca ...
Further on,
José Martí[2]
greets me in passing:

The homeland is an altar, not a pedestal.
                                    January 28, 1968.

Homeland ...
--not of the generals--
it is the blood of the Indians
whose cry clutches at my gut
from the foundation blocks of the Empire State
          Building.
Homeland is the ancestors
of the black people
hunted alive
by the grandfathers of George Washington
and Abraham Lincoln.

Homeland is the blacks
chained together like wild animals
in Dutch ships
who crossed over the ocean
not knowing their destination
and who, like Jesus,
died of thirst,
chained to the mast
of the Cross.

Homeland is the 30,000 Indians
in El Salvador
who died, massacred, in 1932
with the OK of the White House.

---

[1] Santiago Atitlán, Panajachel, Izabal, the Polochic valley, Sayaxche, Parraxtut and Petanac were areas of indigenous resistance and subsequent massacres by the Guatemalan security forces.

[2] José Martí was a 19th century Cuban nationalist who struggled for Cuban independence from Spain.

Patria son los 142 kekchíes
asesinados por el jefe militar
del destacamento
del Oriente,
el 29 de mayo de 1978
en Guatemala
bajo el mandato
del General Kjell Eugenio Laugerud García.

Patria es el sueño de Sandino,
el coraje de Monimbó,
y la herencia de Tupac Amaru.
Patria es el sudor, la agonía, el llanto
y cada gota de sangre de
Yolanda Urízar de Aguilar.

Patria es la respiración asmática del Che
enamorado de la Vida
que hoy recorre incansable
todas las montañas de América,
Es la revuelta de Atanasio Tzul
y el último suspiro de Turcios
y el "vámonos Patria a caminar"
de Otto René...

Patria es el amor al débil
Patria es fraternidad y justicia,
cimiento de la Paz.

Patria es el gemido desgarrador
de Dios en trabajo de parto
salido de la garganta de Jonás
que recorre obediente las calles de Nínive...

Homeland is the 142 Kekchies
assassinated by the commander
of the military's eastern
headquarters
on May 29, 1978
in Guatemala
under the orders
of General Kjell Eugenio Laugerud Garcia.

Homeland is Sandino's[3] dream,
the bravery of Monimbó,[4]
the legacy of Tupac Amaru.[5]
Homeland is the sweat, agony and moaning
and every drop of blood shed by
Yolanda Urizar de Aguilar.[6]

Homeland is Che's asthmatic breathing,
in love with Life
that now sweeps endlessly
through the mountains of the Americas.
It is the revolt of Atanasio Tzul[7]
and Turcios'[8] last breath
and the "Onward, my people!"
of Otto René ...

Homeland is love for the weak
Homeland is brother-sisterhood and justice,
the foundation of Peace.

Homeland is the rending cry
of God in labor
emitted from the throat of Jonah
as he walks obediently in the streets of Ninevah ...

---

[3] Gen. Augusto Cesar Sandino was the famed Nicaraguan resistance leader who fought against the U.S. Marines in the 1920s and 30s.

[4] Monimbó was a town in Nicaragua whose residents led a popular insurrection against the Somoza regime in February 1978.

[5] Tupac Amaru was the last Inca ruler and led the resistance to Spanish conquest in the 1500s.

Patria es el sentir de Jesús,
que siendo igual a Dios,
no se aferró a su rango de Hijo,
sino que vaciado de sí mismo,
se sometió a la voluntad del Padre
menospreciando su vida hasta la muerte.

Patria,
querida hermana rica,
negra o blanca
de los Estados Unidos,
es aceptar el escándalo de la Cruz,
descender del pedestal
de todas tus seguridades económicas
y morir cada día un poco
para que otros puedan vivir.

Sólo entonces
podrás remontar el vuelo
"más que el cóndor y el águila real"
y por encima de todas las torres de Babel
derribarás murallas
de clases,
de razas
y de sexos.
Sólo entonces,
conocerás la libertad
y podrás contribuir
con tu pedacito de justicia
a construir el Mundo Nuevo
donde reinará por fin la Paz.

New Jersey
Junio 16 de 1984

Homeland is the response of Jesus,
who being one with God,
did not cling to his place as Son,
but rather, emptied himself,
submitted to the will of the Father
and humbled himself unto death.

Homeland,
my dear, wealthy sister,
black or white,
from the United States,
means accepting the scandal of the cross,
descending from the pedestal,
leaving all economic securities
and dying a little every day
so that others might live.

Only then
will you ascend again in flight
"higher than the condor and the stately eagle"
and above all the towers of Babel
you will demolish the walls
of class,
race,
and sex.
Only then
will you know liberty,
and will you be able to add
your little bit of justice
to build the New World
where at last Peace will reign.

New Jersey
June 16, 1984

---

[6] Yolanda Urizar de Aguilar was a labor lawyer who was disappeared by Guatemalan security forces.

[7] Atanasio Tzul was a Quiché leader who led a partially successful uprising against Spanish colonial rule.

[8] Luis Turcios Lima was an idealistic Guatemalan army officer who became disillusioned with the use of Guatemalan territory for the staging of the Bay of Pigs invasion of Cuba. He later led an uprising against the Guatemalan government which commenced war for national liberation.

FURTHER READING

Threatened with Resurrection by Julia Esquivel.
The Brethren Press.

Guatemala: Eternal Spring, Eternal Tyranny by
Jean Marie Simon. W.W. Norton and Co.

I, Rigoberta Menchú ed. by Elizabeth Burgos–
Debray. Schocken Books.

Guatemalan Women Speak by Margaret Hooks.
CIIR (Distributed in U.S. by EPICA).

*The Battle for Guatemala: Rebels, Death
Squads, and U.S. Power* by Susanne Jonas.
Westview Press.

Indian Guatemala: Path to Liberation by Luisa
Frank and Philip Wheaton. EPICA.

OTHER EPICA PUBLICATIONS

Guatemalan Women Speak by Margaret Hooks. A collection of interviews with Guatemalan women--peasants, refugees, guerrillas, housewives, politicians, nuns. ($9.95 plus $1.55 postage). 128 pages.

Guatemala: Burden of Paradise by Duncan Green. Illustrated by John Keane. A narrative of the social history of Guatemala with stunning full color artwork. ($12.95 plus $1.55 postage). 64 pages.

Indian Guatemala: Path of Liberation by Luisa Frank and Philip Wheaton. A comprehensive account of the liberation process of the indigenous people. ($6.95 plus $1.55 postage). 112 pages with illustrations.

El Salvador: A Spring Whose Waters Never Run Dry, edited by Scott Wright, et al. A collection of testimonies from the Christian Base Communities gathered over the last ten years. ($6.00 plus $1.50 postage). 96 pages with illustrations.

Death and Life in Morazán: A Priest's Testimony from a War–Zone in El Salvador. ed. by María López Vigil. A first-hand account of daily life in a conflictive zone in El Salvador. ($8.95 plus $1.55 postage). 105 pages.

Condoning the Killing: Ten Years of Massacres in El Salvador. ed. by EPICA. Based on investigations by the Salvadoran Human Rights Commission (non–governmental), this book documents 32 massacres committed by the Salvadoran Armed Forces and raises issues for U.S. policy. ($5.95 plus $1.55 postage).

Challenge: A Journal of Faith and Action in the Americas. Latin American theologians and activists write about their struggle and their faith. ($10.00 annual subscription for 3 issues).

Send orders to:
EPICA o 1470 Irving St. NW o Washington, DC 20010